EXPRESSIVE
INTERIORS

EXPRESSIVE
INTERIORS

HOMES THAT CELEBRATE SELF-EXPRESSION

JO BERRYMAN

photography by Bénédicte Drummond
foreword by Rachel Ashwell

CICO BOOKS
LONDON NEW YORK

For Nico, Romy and Elijah

First published in 2024 by
Ryland Peters & Small
20–21 Jockey's Fields
London WC1R 4BW
and
341 E 116th Street
New York, NY 10029

www.rylandpeters.com

Text copyright © 2024 Jo Berryman
Photography copyright © 2024
Bénédicte Drummond
Copyright © 2024 Ryland Peters & Small

10 9 8 7 6 5 4 3 2 1

ISBN : 978-1-80065-383-2

Designed by Paul Tilby
Senior Commissioning Editor:
Annabel Morgan
Editor: Sophie Devlin
Head of Production: Patricia Harrington
Creative Director: Leslie Harrington

British Library Cataloguing-in-Publication Data. A catalogue record for this book is available from the British Library.

Printed and bound in China.

FSC
MIX
Paper | Supporting
responsible forestry
www.fsc.org
FSC® C008047

CONTENTS

FOREWORD

by Rachel Ashwell

Jo Berryman lives just down the road from me in the English countryside, each of us in our own magical, historical homes. As I began the process of renovating my home, I was massively inspired by the world Jo has created in hers. To me, her decorating style is where rock 'n' roll meets beautiful, brave storytelling and an infusion of pure spiritual energy.

It is clear Jo decorates with confidence from her layering of palettes and textures. She has an eye, a touch and a heart that enable her to compose a gorgeous symphony in which every element belongs and is given space to shine, creating interiors that are an inspiration for all the senses. As I experience and study Jo's work, I come away with lessons learned from her brilliant demonstration of how expressive juxtapositions can create unique and arresting homes.

INTRODUCTION

Take a moment to revisit early 2020. We face a dystopic moment, a bewildering pandemic and subsequent lockdown. A divisive time for humanity. Depending on your perspective, we are either imprisoned or safely ensconced within – and that's if you're lucky enough to have a home. Many see the home for what it really is: hallowed. A temple of certainty in a time of uncertainty. The Crosby, Stills, Nash and Young song *Our House* loops through my head, intimate and hymnal. It embodies the spirit of this book.

Everything is done.
Such a cozy room, the windows are illuminated
By the evening sunshine through them,
Fiery gems for you, only for you.
Our house is a very, very, very fine house.

Every house has the potential to be a very fine house. When I embark on a design process, I kick off with a 'bloom board', my version of a mood board. It's founded on a key image offered up by the client, which can be anything: an artwork, a family photograph or even the concentric rings within a slice of agate. The bloom board helps to frame an inaugural conversation. I liken this part to speed dating, because questions need to be efficient and incisive to identify core likes and dislikes. After this, the deep dive begins. The client and I become a single entity. Detailed visuals undergo rounds of permutations. Conscious of not imprinting my own aesthetic, we find common ground. It's a visceral and intuitive process. Our journey is a dance that starts off as a waltz, trips into a freestyle routine, then circles back to a waltz.

Those who choose to work with me are often aware that my style isn't demure or rule based. I can spout a multitude of tried and trusted theories, but mostly I'm a believer in being true to what you like regardless of whatever's on trend. You like what you like for a reason, and if you start at this baseline the outcome will be original, but more importantly, will endure the test of time. This is particularly resonant now, given the deluge of aspirational, fast-changing imagery on social media. It's easy to lose sight of yourself and succumb to comparisons.

Expressive Interiors celebrates those who seek authenticity over conventionality and meaningful connections over material possessions. Whether arranging photographs and objets d'art with meticulous care or unleashing creativity with the wild abandon of an abstract painter, there are no 'shoulds' here. This book celebrates a sense of self-expression thriving within the sanctuary of one's home. From the east coast of Scotland to Ibiza, my mission is to encourage everyone to decorate without fear of judgement and for the reader to revel in the freedom that ensues.

FUTURE, PAST, PRESENT

Since 1966, families with 'B' surnames have lived at Somerleaze. Mine is Berryman (née Briston) and my husband's is Bergkvist – call it superstition, but we feel like the rightful custodians of our Victorian home in Somerset.

WOVEN TOGETHER
Keen to preserve original architectural elements, we wove them into the design. This fusion of modernity and period features is a theme that runs throughout the house.

HUMBLE GRANDIOSITY
Clad in mountain limestone and bedecked in wisteria, when we saw Somerleaze it was a case of love at first sight. The carriage drive and circular fountain installed by our predecessors lend the house a grandiose quality.

We found our dream home in the wilds of Somerset. On an autumnal afternoon, we knocked at the door like a pair of trick-or-treating teenagers, reluctant players in our very own gothic horror story. We were met with a warm welcome by the owners but a firm no when we gently broached the subject of a future acquisition. Somerleaze House was their continuing opus and, they declared, they would only exit feet first.

It was impossible not to marvel at such unwavering resolve from a pair of octogenarians. A friendship flourished, and we'd often drop in for tea, biscuits and copious pearls of wisdom. Eventually, after a bitter and challenging winter, the owners decided to sell, and we enthusiastically agreed to take the house on.

Somerleaze is a charming hybrid: Victorian bones and a neo-Elizabethan soul. Built in the 1880s, it was designed by ecclesiastical architect CE Giles (who did not live to see its completion) for wealthy merchant George Walters. The main walls are limestone and Beer freestone, while pitched pine, an edgy choice for the time, features throughout.

Our predecessors had downsized from a French chateau and, unashamedly maximalist, had papered and upholstered every surface. As we started peeling back the layers, revelatory scenes appeared. The walls

took on a faded splendour, reminiscent of the walls of the Harley Street consulting room in Tom Hooper's Oscar-winning movie *The King's Speech*. We embraced the imperfection, living with and making good of it. This inclination is embroidered throughout the house and my life. My penchant for creating pockets of neat mess is unbridled. Give me a surface and I'll adorn it with objets, trinkets, books and captivating oddities. Injecting drama and dynamism into spaces is crucial; stagnant surroundings are dull, while a touch of chaos can set the *chi* energy in motion.

The extension was conceived during a lockdown spent with our friend, the chef Tim Siadatan. He found it amusing that the kitchen and utility areas didn't fit with the grandiose proportions of the reception rooms. So much life takes place within these spaces, and we decided to honour that, commissioning award-winning architect Takero Shimazaki to create a vision for the space.

Local materials and craftsmen were employed for the extension with Purbeck stone the bedrock of the design. We worked with Triptych Furniture in Melksham to create finishes to complement the architecture. The design inspiration for this new space was the trees and valleys surrounding the house and their tones are distilled into the palette, which is rich in earthy hues. A *shou sugi ban* finish was applied to the cabinetry, which is coated in a dull gold on the main wall and iron grey on the island. A slab of calacatta macchia vecchia tops the island and forms a waney-edged splashback at one end of the room. The pièce de résistance is the catering-grade extractor fan wrapped in copper and floating above the range cooker. With its rosy patina and opulent curves, it's not just a hood, but a sculpture. As golden hour hits, the kitchen radiates with warm, glowing light.

Our changes took a year to conceptualize and another year to execute; add a pregnancy into the mix and we certainly had our work cut out for us. In a piece of perfect timing, Elijah, my third child, was born just as the extension came to completion.

SUBTLETY VS IRREVERENCE

The dance between two polarities is at play here. A graphic wallpaper by Pierre Frey counteracts the rawness of the stripped-back ceiling, while Joa's White by Farrow & Ball creates the perfect canvas for the plethora of objects and furniture on display. A mid-century Swedish sofa upholstered in a looped alpaca tweed takes centre stage, the coffee table is acid etched and echoes the pleasing circularity of the sofa. In the far corner a vintage Eero Aarnio ball chair sits beside a pair of Eero Saarinen Tulip lamps perched atop a white lacquered sideboard/credenza with mirrored inserts. The Big Bulb chandelier is by CTO Lighting.

MATERIAL WEALTH

In the kitchen, the palette is one of elemental hues: copper, brass, terracotta, iron, ochre, cream and gold. A reeded glazed cabinet breaks up the bulk of the island and lights up at night. The floor is locally sourced Purbeck flags, brushed and tumbled to imperfect perfection. The Bauhaus-inspired copper hood crafted by Simon Hebditch of Inspired Metal is flanked by two Artes Sconces by CTO Lighting.

EARTH TO TABLE
The long oak table is surrounded by bespoke chairs in Ultrafabric pleather. A former doorway has been transformed into bookshelves and the lantern is by CTO Lighting. The dried flower installation is by floral artist Sarah Jayne Edwards

NICHE INTEREST
A beloved abstract acrylic found at Shepton Flea and a sculpture by Andrew Hewish are neatly ensconced within the frame of a former window.

SEAT WITH A VIEW
An original William Andrus for Steelcase armchair overlooks the landscape. Behind, a 1950s Italian Diabolo floor lamp provides ambience at night.

THINKER'S HAVEN

As we peeled away layers of wallpaper in the library and study, we uncovered an unexpected treasure: a plaster finish of exquisite hue. The floors were stripped and stained with Liberon wood dye. The lips captured by Hervé Dunoyer, a renowned beauty photographer, deliver sensual provocation alongside the practicality of a library unit—once a resident in London's Swiss Cottage Library. The room is anchored by a Drapers Table by Rose Uniacke and timeless original Hans Wegner wishbone chairs.

LAYERED BOUDOIR

A 1950s Italian sofa upholstered in milk chocolate suede and draped in green mohair wool sits at one end of the main bedroom. The walls are painted in Farrow & Ball's Peignoir, a whisper of pink enveloped in a plume of smokey grey. The framed Madonna is an eBay find, no doubt plundered from some unknown Italian church.

'Somerleaze is a charming hybrid: Victorian bones and a neo-Elizabethan soul.'

BUILT-IN CHARM
A Battenberg configuration of units crafted by local cabinet makers Triptych Furniture. The facades are sprayed cobalt blue, soft clay, pale blush and pistachio and embellished with a rose gold inlay and drawer pulls. The 19th-century French giltwood chair is upholstered in Les Rocheuses linen by Pierre Frey.

SPARE APPARENT
The two-tone walls are rendered in a deeply pigmented lime wash by Kreidezeit. The bespoke headboard is clad in a vegan indigo suede by Schumacher and flanked by a pair of 1950s walnut veneer, mirror-topped side tables.

SOARING HEIGHTS

Confronted with the limitations of a small room, our gaze turns upwards (*opposite*). A feature wall is adorned in a verdant oak-leaf motif wallpaper from Pierre Frey. Central to this lofty scheme is the bespoke headboard, its baroque curves studded with large bronze buttons and wrapped in a textured weave by Romo. The vaulted ceiling panels are stained oak, the floor is painted in Farrow & Ball's Cornforth White and the walls in tranquil Peignoir. The nursing chair is Victorian vintage and dressed in a Medici blue velvet with matching fringe. The nude is by David Cobley.

RITUALS

A bath from The Albion Bath Company has centre stage upon a Carrara marble platform. The intention here was to evoke the ceremony of Roman baths, where water equated to cleanliness and spiritual renewal.

MATERIAL WEALTH

A bateau bath is sprayed in burnished iron and a bejewelled Kasbah chandelier hangs resplendent above, its light casting patterns that dance across the room, turning a bath into a magical and restorative event.

PLAYING WITH SCALE

I revel in the unexpected, and pairing the bold with the understated creates a dialogue between elements that don't typically converse. Picture a lofty, minimal room where a tiny, ornate antique clock sits on a stark white mantle. Such scale play draws the eye, piquing curiosity and the conjuring of stories about the clock's past lives.

An oversized headboard, assertive and dominant in a small space, strikes a note of grandeur. Similarly, a large black and white photograph threatening to break the confines of a narrow wall or a polished piece set against a rough textural backdrop, creates visual drama. Bold juxtapositions that challenge and redefine traditional aesthetics create interest within a scheme.

My background in fashion influences the way I approach interiors. Just as a statement necklace transforms a plain white t-shirt, I use standout pieces

like an oversized, sculptural lamp or a cluster of intricate frames to add personality to a room. It's about finding the balance where each piece complements and highlights the others, like the accessories that pull an outfit together.

Each decorative choice is a deliberate stroke in the painting of a room's story. Each element plays a role, resulting in beguiling vignettes that encourage reflection and an appreciation of wit and detail.

The conversion from ecclesiastical building to home was masterminded by West Architecture under the skilled guidance of Graham West and Hana Ichikawa. Their distinctive application of timber, steel, resin and brick forms the foundational palette. Split into two levels, the home comprises two bedrooms, an indulgent bathroom and an expansive open-plan living space. The soaring ceiling height and classical arched windows exalt the main living space and drench it in natural light. A gravity-defying stairway with a sculptural silhouette connects the different levels and sets the architectural tone.

João has furnished the space with pieces from his own collection that echo the soft

Studio 3, formerly a 19th-century Methodist church in London's Islington, is home to designer João Botelho and his beloved cocker spaniel, Oscar. Following a separation, João was looking to downsize. The hunt seemed fruitless until a fortuitous flurry of events led him to this property. It was love at first sight.

NOUVEAU DECO

angles and streamlined curves of Art Deco yet wholeheartedly embrace the 21st century. His use of luxurious materials and richly hued fabrics balances the minimalist backdrop. Lighting by Schwung, home accessories dating back to his glamorous days working alongside Donna Karan in New York and an arresting art collection, including photography by Thomas Zanon-Larcher and abstract paintings by Manoel Bersan, infuse the space with a mood of culture, energy and elegance.

João's love for green permeates the scheme, creating an ambient and harmonious backdrop that's inspired by the lushness of the Amazon rainforest, testament to his Brazilian roots and zest for life. Lofty fig trees, frothy ferns, cascading climbers and a scattering of succulents offset the bouclé, natural weaves and velvets in a spectrum of verdant shades.

Mirrors of varying sizes and shapes are strategically positioned throughout to reflect the beauty of the scheme and amplify the natural light. The majestic mezzanine, canopied above the kitchen, accommodates a self-contained guest bedroom, complete with oversized mirror, luxurious bed, cascading plants and lush banana tree. Sultry

MOSS BOSS
The Zeus Sofa from Casa Botelho takes centre stage (*opposite*). Deeply set and plush, it is forged with brass detailing and upholstered in a mossy hued bouclé fabric. A circular rug with striking onyx border by Tapis Studio defines the main living area.

URBAN RETREAT
Wall-to-wall bespoke cabinetry provides extensive storage while a circular mirror reflects the light coming in through the multiple arched windows (*right*). The steel staircase offers ample opportunity for plant hanging and creates shady pockets for ferns and statement planters.

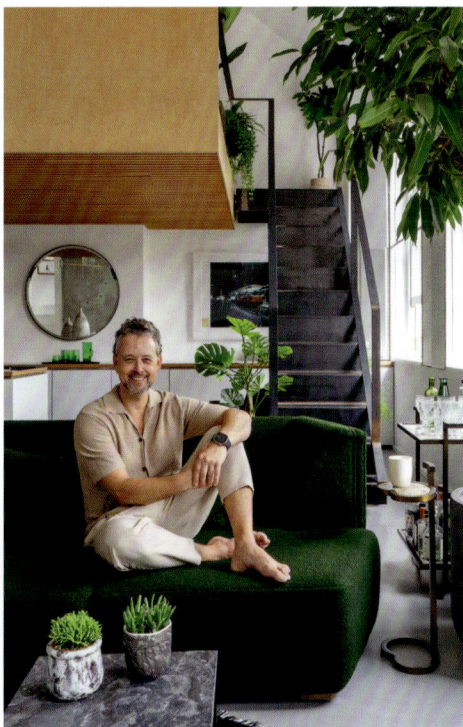

black and white photographs by Christopher Pillitz adorn the walls, imbuing the space with the nostalgic mood of the Tango.

The main bedroom, enveloped in a birchwood cocoon, is an ode to timber, soothing neutrals and a minimalist aesthetic. Black and white photography punctuates the scene. The low-level timber bed and clever blackout shutters ensure the deepest of sleeps. A floating bioethanol fireplace serves as a monochrome centrepiece, its sleek, unobtrusive design fitting seamlessly into the room's aesthetic, offering a source of warmth without disrupting its minimalist shell. The firelight casts subtle shadows against the backdrop, a flickering light play similar to that of an immersive art experience.

The bathroom is a continuation of the minimalist theme. A handsome claw-footed roll-top bathtub is positioned beneath a

perfectly placed skylight, creating an idyll for relaxation and introspection. A melange of trinkets, potions, objets d'art and yet more greenery adorns the surfaces, adding a layer of sophistication.

Studio 3 is more than just a live/workspace. Here, João can conceive designs, develop ideas and showcase his stylish wares, all within an environment that not only fosters creativity but promotes tranquil living.

VITA-MIX

The modern state-of-the-art kitchen utilizes compressed MDF for the countertop and has a slatted birchwood ceiling that forms the underside of the mezzanine, injecting a pleasing linear repeat and showcasing a floating strip light by Schwung Lighting. The dining table, bench and chairs are all by Casa Botelho. Clean white units contrast with the industrial stainless-steel surface, a noiseless backdrop for Thomas Zanon-Larcher's cinematic photography. Indoor plants enliven the scene.

CLEAN CANVAS

A Casa Botelho armchair sits back to back with its matching footstool, alongside a family of inky black occasional tables. The brass chandelier is by Schwung Lighting. This is the ideal viewing point for Manoel Bersan's contemplative abstract and Thomas Zanon-Larcher's photographs. The staircase leads up to João's studio.

BEST GUEST

A trio of photographs by Christopher Pillitz add dynamism to the guest bedroom on the mezzanine level (*left*). An oversized mirror by Casa Botelho rests against the wall and bounces daylight into the space.

BOUTIQUE STAY

A mustard-clad Atena armchair and lush banana tree on the glazed mezzanine (*opposite*). The original brickwork, a reminder of the building's age and origins, adds texture to the pared-back palette. A pair of adjustable, forged brass floor lamps illuminate the space while the luxurious bed ensures that João's guests experience a boutique hotel-like stay.

'João's use of luxurious materials and richly hued fabrics balances the minimalist backdrop.'

SWEET DREAMS

In the main bedroom, architectural and interior design elements join forces to create a serene space that's conducive to the deepest of sleep. Birchwood timber wraps around the space, creating a dreamy cocoon. Neat lips and ledges are integrated into the design, allowing for display of a cinematic still photograph by Thomas Zanon-Larcher. The low-level bed is luxurious yet minimalist and the floating fireplace adds extra warmth and focal interest.

ACCENT REPETITION

Repetition of decorative accents plays a pivotal role in establishing harmony and cohesion within an interior. The concept revolves around the deliberate repetition of specific elements, such as colours, patterns, motifs, textures or shapes throughout a room, or even a whole home, to create a pleasing sense of unity and cohesion.

One of the easiest ways to implement this technique is through colour. For example, a particular shade can be picked out in paint, a throw, cushions, rugs, curtains and artwork, weaving a visual narrative that connects rooms throughout the entire house. A tonal scheme based on various shades in the same hue will create a dramatic effect. In our kitchen, I painted the ceiling the same burnt orange tone as the dining chairs to produce an enveloping canopy of colour and interesting trajectory for the eye as it bounces around the space.

Pattern and texture offer another dimension for accent repetition. Try introducing a specific pattern or shape on one element, such as a sofa, then repeating it in a subtler way on cushions or a feature wall. Similarly, textures provide a decorative thread. Upholstering a bedroom wall in the same fabric as the headboard, or applying a tadelakt finish to a shower room for a Moroccan spa-like feel, then employing the same finish on the kitchen wall serves to build in a tactile experience that creates harmony throughout a home.

PATTERN POETRY

A Georgian house on the east coast of Scotland is home to Wendy Morrison, a fashion-turned-rug designer. She lives here with her husband, their two boys and the menagerie: Eddie the dog, chickens and ducks. Wendy's work with colour has brought all her visions to life.

The family had previously lived in France, close to the border with Switzerland. On their return to the UK, a friend was leaving to spend time overseas and an opportunity to rent her farmhouse presented itself. The Morrisons moved in and fell hard for the woodland setting and the limitless lifestyle potential they discovered. They asked their friend if she was up for selling, and the answer was yes.

Wendy has plans to relocate the kitchen to the dining room, but so far renovations have been minimal. Instead, the house is staged as an evolving backdrop for social media and magazine features to showcase her exquisite rug and wallpaper designs. These efforts have significantly contributed to the growth of her business, which is enjoying global success.

Although the property is situated in a town, the woodland garden gives it a bucolic feel. It wraps around the house in an L-shape, making the most of the sunlight due to its southwesterly aspect. The outdoors is a continuation of the living space, especially during the spring and summer months. There's a walled garden to the east that's accessible from the kitchen and home to the family's chickens and ducks.

Inside, large windows bring sunshine into the interior. This was originally painted in pale tones with a dark woodwork/trim, but has morphed into a kaleidoscopic dreamscape filled with patterns and contrasts, an actualization of Wendy's wonderland.

A porch entrance opens onto a long corridor with a black-painted floor and a Cole & Son Rousseau border on the walls. The traditional kitchen was built bespoke years ago and has a convivial round table at its heart. A more formal dining set-up in a separate room is where the family eat their evening meals, with vintage cabinetry displaying collections of table and glassware.

The spacious living room overlooks the garden, its walls adorned with Wendy's Mandela paper and contrasting rich black paint on the picture rail and ceiling. A plush blue velvet sofa is trimmed with bright white piping. Wendy's treasure trove of chinoiserie pieces, including a coffee table with drawers and latticework chairs, infuses the space with her signature aesthetic. Her Talisman hand-knotted rug and hand-embroidered crewelwork tapestries used as curtains add further layers of colour and texture.

The main bedroom, one of four, has plenty of standout architectural features: majestic floor-to-ceiling windows, a high ceiling, deep cornicing and arched alcoves flanking the fireplace, while Wendy's Joie de Vivre wallpaper covers the walls. The family bathroom is no less dramatic, with walls clad in Wendy's Phoenix paper with vivid green wainscotting and a black ceiling to complete the effect. In contrast, the adjacent shower room is a party in pink.

This house is a true reflection of the vibrant family who live within its glorious Georgian architecture. It serves both as a sanctuary and a creative hub, and Wendy's passion for pattern permeates throughout.

CHAMBRE ORIENTALE
Wendy's Joie de Vivre wallpaper and matching rug shimmer in the dappled light (*left*). The vintage French bed has been reupholstered in Osborne & Little's Japanese Garden, with cushions designed in collaboration with Monoprix. The chinoiserie lacquered bedside table/nightstand is from The Nine Schools.

HAPPY LANDING

Upstairs, black and gold bamboo-motif wallpaper harmonizes with a neat chinoiserie bureau and a tasselled lamp from Aquarius Vintage (*above*). A leopard-print tub chair by Accent is paired with a tiger-print pouf from Homesense. Wendy's signature Okinawa circular rug consolidates the look.

THE SNUG COMPANY

In the snug on the ground floor, a leopard-print sofa by House of Sloane is teamed with a Kamachi cushion and Wendy's Eternal Toile wallpaper (*right*). The chinoiserie coffee table makes a fitting contrast with her Eternity Dark rug. The floor lamp is the result of a collaboration with Beauvamp and the oriental vase was found at The Nine Schools.

IN FULL COLOUR

This area is Wendy's work space, where she devises and plans her social media content. Her One Hundred Flowers rug brightens the floor and is paired with matching wallpaper (left). The table and chairs are vintage. The vases were discovered in a salvage yard and the miscellaneous ceramics on the table are from The Nine Schools and TK Maxx.

THE DARK SIDE

Wendy's Peace, Love & Joy rug and Mandela wallpaper set the mood in the family dining room, which is just off the snug and is home to another vintage table and chairs (pages 46–47). The glossy green tasselled lamp was made by Beauvamp using a Coco & Wolf fabric for the shade. The decorative screens are from Drum Farm Antiques and the portrait on the wall is by German artist Olaf Hajek. The highboy came from Wendy's favourite curiosity shop in Edinburgh – she traded it for one of her crewelwork wall hangings.

BLACK IS NEUTRAL

A traditional bathroom has been brought into the 21st century with lashings of vivid green paint and Wendy's Phoenix wallpaper (*above*). A vintage mirror was repainted in off-black and now hangs on the wall above a ceramic pedestal sink by Burlington.

FRESCO BLOSSOM

The hallway is enlivened with a wallpaper border by Cole & Son (*right*). Wendy's Shanghai Blossom rug adds a rainbow layer to the lacquered black floorboards. The ceiling light is by Beauvamp and the leggy demi-lune table was found at Aquarius Vintage. A gilt paper fan procured from a curiosity shop and mounted on the wall adds a final flourish.

EAST MEETS WEST

In the main bedroom, Wendy's Joie de Vivre wallpaper covers the walls and the tasselled ceiling pendant is by London-based studio Coldharbour Lights (*opposite*). The wooden chest of drawers/dresser was a flea-market find.

'The house is staged as an evolving backdrop to showcase Wendy's exquisite designs.'

PATTERN CLASH

Pattern clash has always been my favourite form of rebellion. The mix of conflicting patterns in a single space creates a visual discord that resonates deeply with me. It evokes a dreamy sense of loucheness, reminiscent of 19th-century opium dens in Shanghai or the eclectic installations at the Biba department store in Swinging 60s London.

When executed with conviction, the results are wonderfully wild. Style out a geometric wallpaper with embroidered cushions and a floral rug, connected by a shared palette or complementary themes. Scale and proportion are also key; mixing large patterns with smaller, intricate ones will prevent overwhelm. Then there's the option of breaking with tradition and throwing caution to the wind, swirling everything together in a metaphorical blender to see a unique visual language emerge.

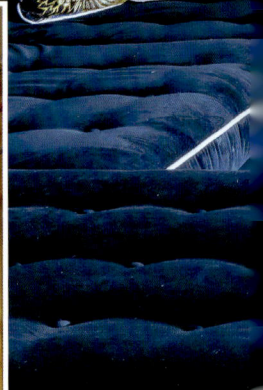

While embracing contrast, my aim is to convey a sense of coherence rather than chaos. Furniture grounds the design and a commitment to using antiques from a specific era or soft furnishings in unifying fabrics can create a cohesive look. A user-friendly method is to start with a neutral canvas and then introduce the pattern clash to break up monotony. Ultimately, this journey is about creativity and personal expression, so I'll avoid being too prescriptive with 'shoulds.' There's a visceral edge and in my experience, when you teeter on this precipice, you often strike gold.

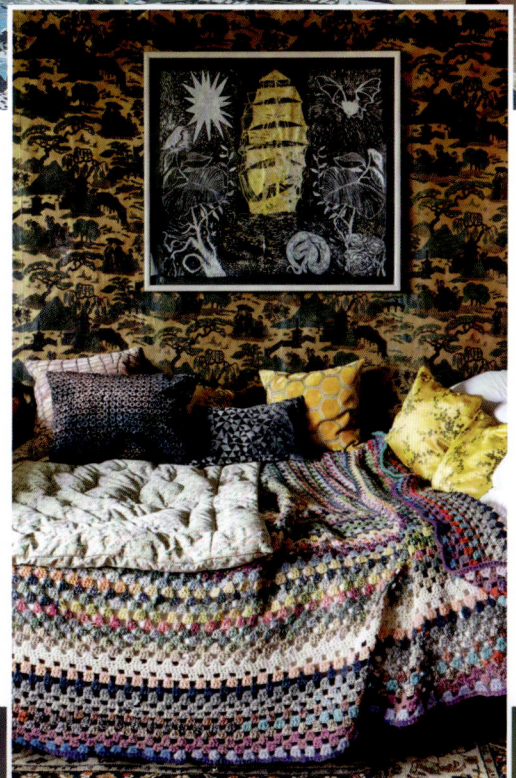

GRANNY'S ATTIC CHIC

In south-east London stands a two-storey late-Victorian maisonette, home to Jamie Watkins and Tom Kennedy, partners in life and in work as the creative duo behind luxury interiors brand Divine Savages. The building's modest exterior belies the vibrant colour and unbridled flamboyance that lies within, wholeheartedly reflecting the brand's identity.

When they first bought the flat, it offered Jamie and Tom more space, better transport links and a garden for their fur babies, Ripley the cat and Newt the miniature Schnauzer. But now, most importantly, it serves as an experimental canvas for their dramatic wallpaper and fabric designs.

After purchase, the couple moved straight in and made the interior habitable. Living and working in the flat through the passing seasons allowed them to study the way in which the light falls and discover which floorboards creaked and where any damp spots lurked. Keen on conserving as much of the original fabric of the building as possible,

they started work on the flat by restoring architectural features such as cornices/coving, picture rails and fireplaces. This in-depth exploration of every inch of their new home sparked a desire to truly imprint their style on the space, and this was the genesis of the Divine Savages wallpaper and fabric brand.

The finished interior reflects the couple's unapologetically maximalist tendencies, and the overall look is a decadent take on a louche boutique hotel. Tom and Jamie have embraced pattern and texture and layered print upon print to glamorous yet playful effect. The maisonette boasts an inviting penny-tiled entrance and a flower-bomb Liberty print stair carpet. The 'kitschen' is embellished with sugar pink zellige tiles, Divine Savages' own Coral Crane Fonda wallpaper and a beloved ceramics collection.

In the living room, a medley of midnight blues provides an inky backdrop for art and taxidermy, with a designated cocktail and dining area defined by their glamorous Deco Martini wallpaper. The bedrooms, meanwhile,

are a fanfare of prints, colours and textures: the main bedroom showcases the opulent, jungly Faunacation wallpaper and an exotic peacock-hued palette, while the guest room features the more subdued Poochi wallpaper, with prancing dogs skipping across a neutral backdrop, and vintage furnishings.

The main bathroom is home to a squid ink-hued Seanic Depths shower curtain and a cabinet of curiosities, while the guest en-suite cleverly integrates wallpaper into the shower for an immersive experience. Tom's collection of curios are displayed throughout, and the couple's joint passion for natural history, kitsch motifs, bold pattern and original features has resulted in a space that's imbued with drama and intriguing detail, steering clear of passing trends.

A shared spirit of wanderlust and the couple's travels through a lush and verdant Bali inspired the landscaping of the pocket-sized garden, an urban oasis that contributes to a balanced work-life dynamic and is also home to a hardworking home studio.

PEACOCK'S TAIL

Peacock-blue hues adorn the main bedroom, where the iconic Divine Savages Faunication jungle wallpaper sets the scene (*right*). A mid-century teak sideboard/credenza is a stage for collected ceramics and objets trouvés. In the foreground, a tantalizing fringed trim embellishes a signature pendant lampshade.

MOODY BLUES

Farrow & Ball's Hague Blue is a striking backdrop for the burgeoning art collection and intriguing objets that surround a deep sofa clad in teal velvet and accessorised with Divine Savages floral cushions.

TALL TALES
A taxidermied peacock commands full attention among a plethora of kitsch artworks and dictates the tone of the room. A tub chair wrapped in velvet perches by the window. The vibrant scheme is grounded by the brick fire surround and roughly hewn wooden floor.

KITSCHEN PARTY Modern white units counteract and calm the explosion of marshmallow pinks in the kitchen (*above*). The zellige tiles, in vertical lay, provide an elegant splashback. The Divine Savages Coral Crane Fonda paper, designed especially to work with the tiles, wraps around the entire kitchen. Against one wall, a vintage shelving unit provides surface space for treasured ceramics and just some of the couple's multitude of collectibles (*right*). A bijou tub sofa covered in an ecru fabric softens and comforts (*opposite*).

'The finished interior reflects the couple's unapologetically maximalist tendencies.'

BLUEDOIR

Divine Savages Faunacation wallpaper and off-black panelling contrast with a vintage metallic bed. The amalgam of bold blues and teals creates a surprisingly serene and restful ambience. A pair of bronze sconces adds a gilded flash and brings out the warm hues within the paper.

FLOCK WORK

The guest suite showcases the Divine Savages Poochi wallpaper, in a tranquil eau-de-Nil shade (*this page and opposite*). Vintage accoutrements complement the subdued tones at play here. The pert pouffe is upholstered in Divine Savages luxurious recycled velvet, while a built-in wardrobe, painted to match the wallpaper, provides storage without taking up too much floorspace (*above*). Clever cabinetry with pigeonhole niches provides additional display space and is home to a charming pair of Staffordshire dogs (*right*). A pair of Poochi print cushions in velvet enliven the faded grandeur of the French bed (*opposite*).

CLUB TROPICANA

Inspired by their travels around Bali and Southeast Asia, Jamie and Tom landscaped the garden and created an idyllic spot to retreat to after a long day's work. Rattan sun loungers dressed in Divine Savages floral cushions bask in the dappled sunlight, surrounded by tropical greenery and an abundance of planters.

GRANNY CHIC

Granny chic brings a nostalgic sense of romance and glamour to an interior. I love to trawl an antiques market or car boot/yard sale imagining what my Granny Vera would have gravitated towards and usually hit the jackpot in bargain bins full of 1960s ceramics, pretty paste or enamel brooches and faded daguerreotypes, all of which look wonderful displayed en masse in a glazed cabinet or pinned to a velvet cushion. Home in on whatever catches your eye. It's like method acting for interiors, can you channel your inner granny?

Staffordshire dogs make charming collectibles, as does high quality taxidermy. Birds, flora, fauna and bugs in boxes always work a treat. If this feels a bit too gruesome, frothy fronds of pampas and plumes of feathers make eye-catching centrepieces. I have a soft spot for kitsch art and botanical prints, offset with modern pieces like a streamlined sofa or zesty floral accents.

Be warned – this look is not for the minimalists among us. There's an art to adding decorative clutter without looking like a hoarder. Be disciplined and don't go overboard with the unexpected. But do have fun arranging intriguing vignettes of flea-market finds, transforming dainy china teacups into candle holders and draping colourful quilts over a bed or armchair.

SEVENTIES REVIVAL

Ensconced within the leafy fringes of London exists an architectural jewel, built in 1970 by architect WSA Williams and inspired by modernist residences of Southern California, designed by the likes of Ray Kappe and Richard Neutra.

This house is home to a vibrant family of four: Jasmine, a wellness expert, author and chef, her partner and co-creator Nick, and their two children, two dogs and a menagerie of inherited fish, local frogs and other wildlife. They decamped here from London's Elephant and Castle, having lived for a decade in a hybrid space that combined both residential and workplace elements. Despite the practicality and edgy allure of this urban lifestyle, a yearning for outdoor space and expansive vistas gradually took hold. The move was eventually sparked by their dogs and a house listing that Nick spotted on his favourite website, The Modern House.

The purchase was not straightforward, but despite the constraints of finance and a bidding war, it seems that the house chose them. A human connection with the sellers, a sense of unwavering persistence when it came to the ups and downs of the buying process and the house's charm all combined to make it inevitable.

The home, predominantly styled with mid-century and seventies retro influences, features an open-plan ground floor with exposed brick walls, chunky concrete lintels and cedar-clad ceilings. Thanks to Jasmine's ongoing and in-depth exploration of Feng Shui and Vastu Shastra, a traditional Hindu system of architecture, the space is imbued with a sense of flow and tranquillity. The main living space is an L-shape configuration wrapped around an internal courtyard. The abundance of glazing allows for a wealth of natural light, whatever the weather or season.

Since moving in, Nick and Jasmine have undertaken various renovations, maintaining the integrity of the house's original design while infusing it with their own personal style. Cork flooring has been laid upstairs, which, quite aside from its hip and retro connotations, is sustainable, durable and water resistant. Each room explodes with a kaleidoscope of colour and idiosyncratic flair. And there is more to come. Plans are brewing to reinstate the original koi carp pond in the inner courtyard, a floating staircase and an indoor garden. Nick and Jasmine continuously draw inspiration from the house's original provenance and their predecessors.

The couple's approach to interior design is eclectic, playful and instinctive, with many treasured pieces accrued over the years.

RETROFÊTE
A 1970s Colin & Hayes modular sofa clad in its original geometric print upholstery, offsets the architectural brick wall and gallery of found artworks (*right*). A 1960s lamp with ruched Murano shade perches upon a vintage copper pedestal side table, beneath which untamed tufts of flame-hued shag pile provide textural play and comfort underfoot.

Jasmine's well-honed eye makes car booting/thrifting look like something of an artform, which is perhaps not surprising given her study of furniture and product design twenty years ago. This home is a treasure trove of mid-century furniture, objets trouvés, important artworks, flea-market acquisitions and holistic design elements that sing in harmony to create a space that is unique.

The segue between indoors and outdoors is seamless. The garden is an integral extension of the living space, thoughtfully zoned with a vegetable patch, nature pond and sun-trap seating area, all of it a sanctuary for family and wildlife.

This home is not just a bricks and mortar structure but an evolving canvas that paints a picture of this family's life, reflecting their deep respect for architecture, history, colour and sustainable living.

'The abundance of glazing allows for a wealth of natural light, whatever the weather or season.'

ART IN RESIDENCE
A beloved commission by Charlotte Keates, renowned for her utopian depictions of interior, architecture and space, sets the tone for the entire house (*opposite*). Beneath sits a utilitarian mid-century chest of drawers, beside it a bamboo plant stand, a fixture of Jasmine's childhood, which she rediscovered in her mother's attic.

BEYOND THE WOOD
A jungle of indoor plants provides verdant contrast to the many wooden surfaces (*right*). The painting on the half-landing is by Alice Grenier Nebout, its colours irradiated by the light cascading through the double-height window.

LIVE VIVID

The vibrant artwork centred above a rosewood sideboard/credenza is by artist Peter Pilgrim (*left*). It caught the couple's eye during a visit to Liberty in London and Nick later tracked it down and purchased the piece directly from the artist for Jasmine's birthday. The G-Plan dining table is underpinned by a classic Berber rug.

EAT CUTE

The kitchen exudes a retro and nostalgic charm thanks to its small dimensions and original tiling and cabinetry (*above*).

LAYER CAKE

The Flowerpot lamps are fitted with Philips Hue bulbs for night-time ambience. An imposing Peter Doig print draws the eye to the Colin & Hayes sofa, now visible in all its glory (*pages 74–75*).

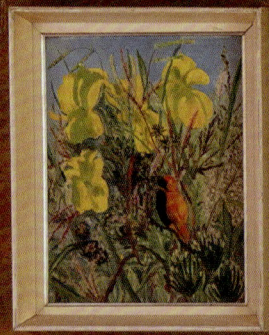

INKY DREAMS
The flood of light in the
bedroom is further amplified
by mirrored built-in storage
(*below*). The walls are Chine
Green by Farrow & Ball. The
original aluminium-framed
windows hark back to the
modernist roots of the house
and offer linear contrast to
furniture and soft furnishings.

'Each room explodes
with a kaleidoscope
of colour and
idiosyncratic flair.'

RATTAN DREAMS
The vintage rattan bed and
inherited oil painting are
fitting accompaniments to the
deep green backdrop. A
sumptuous scatter of cushions
from Caravane and a well-
loved throw add colour (*left*).

OCEAN TILES
The bathroom is adorned in
aquamarine mosaic tiles which
flow seamlessly across all
surfaces (*right*). In keeping
with this aquatic theme is a
pair of bronze goldfish
figurines, placed thoughtfully
on the wall and evoking an
underwater oasis. A 1960s
artwork titled *Nina* by Gerritt
Vandersyde adds a healthy
dose of kitsch.

For me, the magic happens when decorative pieces such as art, ceramics and photos are introduced into a room. In this way, a house is transformed into a home.

Art, in its myriad guises, brings colour, tone and mood to a space. Look for pieces that speak to you in some way. I find myself gravitating towards figurative works by artists such as Alice Instone and Grace O'Connor. If there are budget constraints, rummage through car boot/yard sales, trawl flea markets and scour online auction sites for prints, posters and paintings. Textiles and soft furnishings can also make a bold statement in a room. I love the opulence of devoré velvet, the ephemeral nature of vintage silk or the tactile pleasure of a shearling.

Placement is key to making artwork sing. Hang larger pieces at eye level, anchoring them to seating areas or large pieces of furniture. Create focal points that inspire curiosity, and intrigue and provoke the eye. Smaller spaces, such as halls or staircases, are good spots for a gallery wall showcasing different-sized works. Balance sizes and frames to create drama without the overwhelm.

Make a decorative statement in any room by grouping ceramics, glassware and other treasures in a way that elevates their importance. At home, I drape pearls and VIP backstage passes over a brass belt stand, blending trash and treasure to infuse the space with character. Remember, living spaces are happy ones.

FINCADELIC

Within Ibiza's beating heart and beside a scenic mountainscape lies the home and sanctuary of my dear friend Sophie Daunais. Hailing from Quebec, Sophie's journey has been nothing short of extraordinary.

Sophie embarked on academic adventures in Paris before diving headfirst into the corporate whirlwind of London. It was there, amid bustling city life, that she welcomed her two beautiful children, Oliver and Nova. Together with Matcha, their lovable miniature Dachshund, they make a lively household.

As the children grew, Sophie's yearning for a freer, more adventurous life intensified. The call of Ibiza was irresistible, and soon it became home. Never one to do things by halves, Sophie threw herself into the local community. She established a regenerative agriculture business, birthing a farm-to-table restaurant and gift shop named Juntos. This venture, co-founded with her ex-husband, stands as a testament to their collaborative and harmonious relationship. Together, they've built not just a business, but a beacon of sustainability and local pride.

Sophie's's latest endeavour, avant-garde concept store Parada, is a reflection of her innovative spirit and drive to create and inspire. In every aspect of her life, she is an unstoppable force of nature, continually redefining her world with vigour and grace.

When she found her Ibicencan finca home, it was a glorious ruin dating back to the early 20th century. Sophie is passionate about preserving the island's architectural heritage, so materials including sabina wood, stone and rendered plaster were used in the renovation alongside modern design elements. An abundance of herbs grow on the land, along with olive trees and a flourishing stone fruit orchard. Sophie is a foodie and apothecarist at heart, and makes syrups and infusions from the surrounding bounty.

Inside, state-of-the-art appliances sit next to reclaimed doors, ceramics, timber and artisanal ironwork. Windows, skylights and fireplaces abound, flooding the house with light and warmth. Ibiza's balmy climate allows for a great deal of outdoor living, and during the summer months, the indoors and outdoors spaces blur into one.

Handmade Moroccan tiles and a picture window overlooking an olive tree welcome visitors. The kitchen is bright and practical, with marble, metal work and weathered wood incorporated into the design. An imposing Lacanche oven takes centre stage and there

SOFT CURVES
Natural textiles and exquisite tapestries, like theses one by Finnish artist Kustaa Saksi, add softening layers to the rendered shell of the building (*opposite*). There are no linear edges here, everything undulates and curves, including like stairs and door architraves.

is children's art on the walls and an inviting breakfast spot at the kitchen island. Sophie even has a secret dining room tucked away in the pantry for intimate dinner parties. The house is filled with many such playful surprises.

The living room exudes earthiness and pared-back luxury. A tapestry by Kustaa Saksi hangs above the dining area, depicting hummingbirds, owls, mushrooms, crystals and moon phases, all imagery Sophie is deeply connected to. A geometric cloud suspended in space by Tomás Saraceno refracts daylight as it falls through a skylight, casting a mesmerising rainbow on the walls.

The main bedroom is centred around *Moonrise*, a hypnotic Billy Childish painting, its watery, lichen-hued palette evoking calm contemplation. In the adjoining bathroom, the organic curves of the bathtub sit below a large picture window and crystals have been embedded into the shower walls, for wellness and a sprinkling of mysticism. The children also have protective totems integrated into the design of their bedrooms, as well as personal shrines to display cherished and meaningful objects.

'The living room exudes earthiness
and pared-back luxury.'

A ROOM FOR ALL SEASONS
Sleek furniture by Danish design company
&Tradition furnishes the main living room. This
cosy space manages to be both warm in the winter
months and cool in the summer. Diaphanous linen
drapes hang at the windows, which lead to an
outdoor seating area. The seasonal flowers are by
Francesca at the Floral Studio in Ibiza.

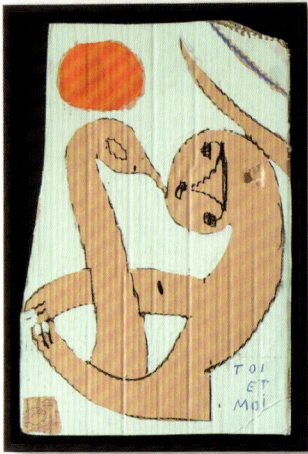

DAILY ART

A Carlito Dalceggio painting on board provides a swatch of colour in the bathroom, where a rustic milking stool perches below colourful hammam towels by Mungo arranged haphazardly on a built-in Vola towel rail, demonstrating how art can emerge from chaos.

ON THE TILES

A vintage lantern is suspended above the tiles in the hallway, which were crafted by artisans in Morocco (*opposite*). A pair of Olafur Eliasson glazed artworks rest on wooden plinths, flanking the rustic bench and picture window.

A pair of Andreas Eriksson paintings command attention above the record player, which sits above a well-stocked vinyl library for moments when an impromptu desire to dance takes hold. The picture window showcases seasonal changes to the landscape. A Nordic folk blanket by SCP adds a burst of pink and purple to the sofa while a shaggy Berber rug warms up the polished concrete floor.

RISE AND SHRINE

Sophie and her family weave spiritual practices into their day, honouring each other, the land and nature. A domestic altar is housed within this niche, holding candles, talismans, charms, symbols, feathers and scribbled notes from loved ones.

ARTFUL EFFECTS

Two exquisite artworks hold this space beautifully (*opposite*). The diffusion of pink light is by German artist Matti Braun and the geometric clouds suspended from the ceiling are by Argentinian artist Tomás Saraceno. The weathered sabina wood beams add contrast to the creamy shell of the building.

COMMUNION
This bespoke rosewood dining table is one of many places to break bread with family and friends. Another epic Kustaa Saksi tapestry hangs above the banquette and vibrates with energy. Sophie connects deeply to the animal and plant symbology depicted here.

'Sophie was passionate about preserving the island's architectural heritage, so sabina wood, stone and rendered plaster were used alongside modern elements.'

RUSTIC MOOD
The kitchen features weathered oak cabinetry and thick cuts of cacao-hued ombra di Caravaggio marble on the worksurfaces (*left*), while the bathroom is home to a deep trough tub and a double vanity made from the same oak (*bottom*).

MOONRISE SLUMBER
Moonrise by Billy Childish sets the palette in the bedroom (*below*). Behind the work is a wall of wardrobes in a woven rattan finish.

OUTDOORSY
The stone terraces with their leafy canopies create ideal outdoor living zones (*right*), and a long Baxter table and chairs provide an idyllic lunch spot. A ceramic totem by acclaimed fashion designer and installation artist Antonio Marras watches benevolently over Sophie's house and land (*above*).

LIVE SEASONALLY

The passing seasons present us with an opportunity to rearrange furniture, cycle colour schemes, and declutter. I thrive during such periods of change, and they profoundly influence my interior design choices.

In colder months, the focus is on more intimate living arrangements, clustering seating around a fire or other heat source as we instinctively move towards smaller spaces that are easily warmed. Richly hued palettes come into play and I layer rugs and throws and light candles as the urge to retreat within the cave takes hold.

The advent of warmer months invokes an 'out with the old, in with the new' mindset as we seek uplift and renewal. In springtime, I hanker after diaphanous fabrics and lighter colours to evoke the sense of expansion we all desire after hibernation. At this time of year our minds turn to maximizing our exposure to natural light, being outside in nature and a seamless

interchange between indoor and outdoor living.

Eating outdoors is one of the joys of the summer months, so make the most of any outside space with a dining table and chairs or a circle of loungers around a fire pit. Outdoor bathrooms are a privilege afforded to those dwelling in sunny climes. If your space is limited, plant climbers on exterior walls, with scented roses and aromatic herbs in pots. Add a hammock or swing chair to a courtyard or balcony and festoon the space with string lights or lanterns

Those without outside space can observe the changing seasons from a serene nook indoors. Position a floor cushion or chaise in a sun-drenched corner and surround it with house plants for a leafy, close-to-nature feel.

SUBURBAN MAXIMALISM

Hidden within a leafy enclave, moments from the cosmopolitan din of Hampstead high street in North London, stands an elegant 1920s semi. White-rendered and iron-gated, it is home to Rosie, Oliver, their two boys and beloved dog Bobbie.

KITCHEN CONFIDENTIAL Simon Hebdditch of Inspired Metal sculpted the brass breakfast bar (*opposite*). Black Bertoia bar stools with coral seats add an Italianate flourish. The gilded mirror surfaces were added by Dominic Schuster.

Rosie, a veritable Wonder Woman born and raised in Singapore, came to London to study law and practised as a lawyer for 14 years. She now offers pro bono legal aid to a cancer charity while simultaneously retraining to be a counsellor and pilot a plane. She also has a magpie's gift for sourcing art and curios. Oliver, a proud northerner and possessor of the most enviable collection of trainers/ sneakers, is a partner in a law firm.

The family moved in on day two of the official lockdown in 2020 and I engaged with the project the minute they got the keys. This is the second home I've helped Rosie and Oliver pull together. This time, they longed for lateral living for their growing boys and surface space for their art collection. Although we couldn't meet in person, we started scheme dreaming using floor plans, virtual tours and photographs.

The first round of changes was cosmetic. The house was a white shell and needed a colour makeover befitting the personality of

its occupants, so we plundered paint archives for non-toxic yet impactful shades. Mountains of sample pots were sent, but an even bolder palette was brewing on the sidelines.

Amid the grimness of the news headlines, this project was pure tonic for the soul as I escaped into paint colour spectrums and devoured digital brochures. When you work remotely, your gaze is irrefutably objective. It became clear to me that the house could take on more colour, pattern and bombastic furniture. When restrictions were finally lifted, a full-throttle offensive began on the house, with architects Thompson + Baroni working alongside us on the structural elements.

On arrival, you first encounter an imposing, serpentine staircase that curves its way to the top of the house. An ethereal Nimbus chandelier by CTO Lighting bathes the hallway in an iridescent glow. Rainer Lagemann's intriguing steel climbing sculptures ascend a cathedral-height wall as you enter into the kitchen, which is a blend of modern

98

design and functionality. Initially designed by Poggenpohl, it has been souped up with new appliances, an antique mirrored splashback and freshly sprayed cabinetry. The reconfigured island serves as a hub for family meals, illuminated by three pendant orbs. A separate room off the kitchen presents an ageless Eero Saarinen set-up for formal dining.

The main living area is a testament to Rosie and Oliver's love of refinement with a dash of irreverence. The walls, clad in a graphic Pierre Frey wallpaper, complement the sophisticated armchairs and jewel-toned sofa set around the modernist marble fire surround. The rug is a floral colour bomb designed by artist Jan Kath. Every piece has been carefully selected to demonstrate the family's ongoing love affair with art and colour.

The master bedroom radiates with softness and light, enhanced by a lustrous built-in wardrobe/closet with bespoke rose-gold doors and decadent puddle-drop curtains that frame the window. The eldest boy is mad for tennis, so his room features a retro tennis-racket wallpaper and vivid ikat patterning on the headboard.

The design themes within the house spill out onto an Italianate walled courtyard garden, which encompasses numerous staggered entertainment zones and a lush lawn for the odd five-a-side football match. The outdoor space is a seamless extension of this creative family home.

EVERYTHING GOES
An ostrich-feather lamp by A Modern Grand Tour
stands between Knoll's Platner easy chair in blue
corduroy and an Amy Somerville sofa in peacock
velvet. The diaspora of colour is underpinned by a
From Russia With Love rug by Jan Kath.

DINNER SERVICE
Eero Saarinen's Tulip table and
chairs sit atop a mohair carpet by
The Rug Company. Curtains in
Pierre Frey's graphic Wokabi print
clash jubilantly with their tangerine
pleather trim. A Roy Lichtenstein
print pulls your gaze towards the
kitchen units, which have been
sprayed in Earthborn's Azalea and
Farrow & Ball's De Nimes.

BOUDOIR BEDROOM
A headboard covered in Adao Verde ombré velvet by Pierre Frey captivates against the kimono-weave wallpaper in celadon (*left*). A pair of 1950s nightstands perch either side of the bed, while a copper and opaline glass pendant from the same era casts a halo diffusion when lit. Infusions of blush are delivered through the rosy hued scatters, copper accents and timber finishes.

SURFACE DETAIL
Watson & Gabb created the wall of wardrobe/closet doors (*above*). The gesso finish is a soft rose gold, lacquered and finely cracked. The windows are framed by curtains fashioned out of a Neisha Crosland velvet, lined and puddle dropped for density and theatre.

ARTFULLY ARRANGED
Rosie's eye for playful art
pervades throughout (*left*).
A satirical piece by Tiggy
Ticehurst, appropriately hung
above a tiger-print
chaise longue, always elicits
a giggle upon waking.

EARTH AND STONE
Terracotta sinks by Cast
Concrete sit on units built out
of travertine with distinctive
markings formed by the
evaporation of water (*above*).
The tiltable bronze mirrors are
from Balineum and the wall
lights are Tom Dixon. Creamy
terrazzo floor tiles bring
in flecked warmth and a hint
of retro madness.

'The master bedroom radiates with softness and light.'

TILE CLASH

Bert & May tiles in royal blue and iron monochrome sing a harmoniously discordant tune in this bathroom (*left*). Nautical Sigvard Bernadotte sconces have been mounted onto the mirrored cabinet to complement the inky-black vanity console.

PRETTY IN PINK

A sweet solution to a storage impasse in a small guest bedroom is to channel the 1980s and incorporate the headboard into a wardrobe/closet niche (*opposite*). This one was crafted by local cabinetmakers AGA Joinery and has plenty of shelving on which to display ceramics and glass. A pair of cushions in Lewis & Wood's Hawksmoor fabric are a fitting accompaniment to the pink paintwork.

HARMONY AND DISCORD

In interior design, harmony and discord dance a delicate waltz. Harmony, that gentle whisper of consistency, manifests through the careful repetition of colours, textures and forms. Imagine a room where a tsunami of muted blues and grays sweeps through, each hue a precursor for the next. Discord can breathe life into an otherwise predictable narrative: a flicker of red in a sea of neutrality or an avant-garde sculpture against a frescoed wall.

For harmony and discord to synergize, I adhere to the following tenets: match eras of furniture – my repertoire spans mid-century, modernist, futuristic 1960s and 70s pattern play – and be consistent in the use of textures – delicate silks, tactile velvets and fuzzy mohairs. Consider these the baseline upon which you can layer discordant notes.

My go-to is pattern clash, a simple and impactful tool, but you can also pair old and new, sleek and rough, high art and kitsch. Asymmetry steps in, breaking monotony with off-kilter charm and teetering on the edge of balance. It's all about artful moderation and choice application, and far from haphazard. You know you're on to something when the note of discord enhances rather than disrupts.

ARTFUL MYSTICISM

In a historic property near Rye, on the edge of Romney Marsh, Alice Instone lives with her husband Hugh, two children, a dog, three cats, nine hens, peacocks and bees.

The property, a rambling farmhouse with outbuildings repurposed into studios for her diverse artistic pursuits, reflects Alice's deep-rooted connection with her surroundings. There are expansive gardens, ancient fruit trees and heavenly pockets of nature all cared for by Alice and her husband.

Alice is a visual artist, known for her powerful and evocative work. She has collaborated with significant cultural figures such as Annie Lennox, Secretary-General of the Commonwealth of Nations Baroness Scotland and scientist Professor Baroness Greenfield. Her projects have graced prominent settings, including the United Nations headquarters in New York, the British Houses of Parliament, Tate Modern and the iconic Hollywood hotel Chateau Marmont. Alice's work is widely renowned, with a string of acclaimed exhibitions. Her most recent accolade was winning Best Fantasy Film at the Cannes Short Film Festival for her film *Oracle*.

The house itself is a fascinating amalgamation of architectural styles spanning several centuries and featuring medieval, Tudor and Queen Anne elements, plus a cluster of Georgian outbuildings. Materials including Kentish ragstone, Tudor brick and wattle and daub tell the story of the building's long and vivid history. A playful tension between vintage and modern is rife; there are 1960s interventions by a Danish architect and contemporary contributions from designers such as Terence Conran.

Alice's connection to the past is palpable not only in her conservation of the physical aspects of her home but also through her approach to household objects. She advocates the use of existing materials and objects, preferring restoration and reuse over replacement in an attempt to preserve a sense of history and craftsmanship. The interior of the house is testament to this philosophy, adorned with antiques, artworks, beloved heirlooms and designs painted by Alice herself.

The property is riddled with intriguing historical scrawlings, including Jacobean witches' marks to ward off evil, Napoleonic graffiti and Victorian doodles, all of which

GILT TRIP
A vintage giltwood tub chair still dressed in its original upholstery is the perfect napping spot for beloved pup Sybil, while a giltwood occasional table stands at its side (*left*). A Gustavian grandfather clock stoically bears witness in the corner. Alice's home is a trove of flea-market acquisitions and found treasures. Almost nothing new crosses her threshold and favoured items are repurposed and restored.

provide a fascinating glimpse into its storied past. All these elements complement the artistic life that flourishes here, where the old milking shed has been transformed into a studio, a forgotten spinning wheel sits in the attic cupboard and sherry bottles left by previous occupants are buried in the floor.

Alice's home is a dynamic space that reflects her artistic ethos and her commitment to blending creativity with historical preservation. The house is an ever-evolving pot on a potter's wheel, moulded by the hands and vision of its owner, serving both as a sanctuary and a source of inspiration. This harmonious blend of past and present in Alice's life underpins her profound connection to her art and her environment.

GET CONNECTED

Alice concocts all her own wall paints. She mixes as she goes along and loves the varying tones that emerge from this process. The entrance hall is enshrouded in a vivid shade of blue, a striking contrast with the pristine white ceiling. The chequerboard tiles bring an Alice in Wonderland-type enchantment. The painting hanging on top of the antique French tapestry is by the artist Ansel Krutt.

In the sitting room, a mesmerising piece by Alice entitled *Night Swim* adorns the wall above the chartreuse velvet sofa (*left*). The walls are embellished with a gilded leaf motif, also painted by Alice. The other end of the room (*pages 116–117*) features two paintings by Scottie Wilson a Scottish-Jewish 'outsider' artist collected by Dubuffet and Picasso. These 20th-century pieces were previously owned by Alice's great aunt, a pioneering child psychiatrist, and adorned her Harley Street consulting room.

KITCHEN AID
Alice restored and repainted the kitchen, upgrading it with appliances and integrated storage. The tomato-red Aga is the heart of the room. The little green landscape painting is by Charlotte Molesworth, the celebrated gardener, who is a huge inspiration to Alice. Charlotte and her husband Donald live nearby and have become firm friends. The tiny white feet on the kitchen table are by Alice.

SEEING RED
A well-loved poster by David Hockney for *The Rake's Progress* rests upon a shelf (*above*). Alice has owned it for years and finally saw the opera with his set designs at Glyndebourne in 2023. Hockney was there in the flesh, which made the experience doubly thrilling. Artist Fiona Banner gifted Alice the *Black Tulip* print for her birthday. This painted blue box was chanced upon by Alice while travelling with Hugh in Stockholm (*opposite*). The shrunken gold head is one of a series of totems that she made for her last show, while the exquisite Japanese kimono is a vintage treasure that has been reappropriated as a wall hanging.

121

PANE, AMORE E FANTASIA

Dried flora and fauna are festooned from the vaulted ceiling in the drawing room. The wreath was decorated by a dear friend, floral artist Tamsin Scott, while the painting is by Alice and dates to a residency at the Chateau Marmont. It's her favourite piece from a series called *I Want to Leave a Souvenir of my Life* – a quote by Italian actress Gina Lollobrigida. The mirrored tabletops were crafted for Alice's 2023 show *A Visit to the Oracle*.

LIVING WALLS

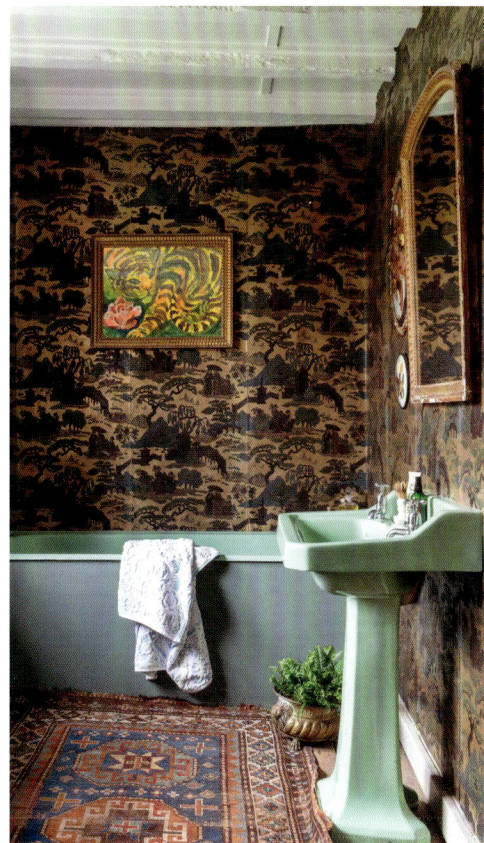

The bedroom walls and lampshades were painted by Alice with a snaking vine motif reminiscent of the tale of Sleeping Beauty (*left*). Layered oriental rugs upon a weathered floor ground the colourful scheme, adding comfort and warmth. The hand-painted four-poster bed is vintage.

SPLASH LANDING

In son Arlo's bathroom, original Victorian wallpaper contrasts majestically with the retro eau-de-Nil bathroom suite (*above*).

THE PRINCESS AND THE BEE

Alice commissioned her talented friend David Hall to create a whimsical box bed fashioned out of lots of old doors for her daughter Bee. The floral curtain, quilt and cushions are all vintage and were hand-sewn either by friends or by Alice herself.

CONNECTING SPACES

I always see beauty in unsung or forgotten 'in-between' spaces and harbour respect for those parts of a home that tend to be an afterthought when decorating. These connecting or linking spaces – foyers, halls, corridors, stairways – wend their way through the heart of a building. Just as a room possesses its own personality and purpose, these liminal spaces can introduce depth and interest to a home.

Whether it's through architectural elements, curated design or furniture arrangement, bringing these spaces into the decorative fold relies on fostering a thread of continuity to create a cohesive whole. A vivid floral carpet or runner will add life and colour to an internal staircase that connects different floors, while mirrored panels make a narrow hallway feel expansive and double the light. Create welcome points by placing an armchair and wall hanging on a landing or a narrow console table adorned with personal treasures in a sliver of hallway.

One solution to a awkward corridor or stairway is a lush and deeply pigmented paint colour paired with a statement light fitting, while a lofty hallway needs nothing more than impactful lighting and bold art. We spend little time in these connecting spaces, so instead of leaving them to straddle the gap between aesthetics and function, why not shine a spotlight upon them and reimagine them as starlets in their own feature?

PLAYFUL OPULENCE

Located on a hill between Ibiza Town and Santa Eulalia, boasting panoramic vistas across the island from sunrise to sunset, is the elegant home of philanthropist and entrepreneur David Leppan. It lies in a semi-rural setting, the holy grail in terms of seclusion and accessibility.

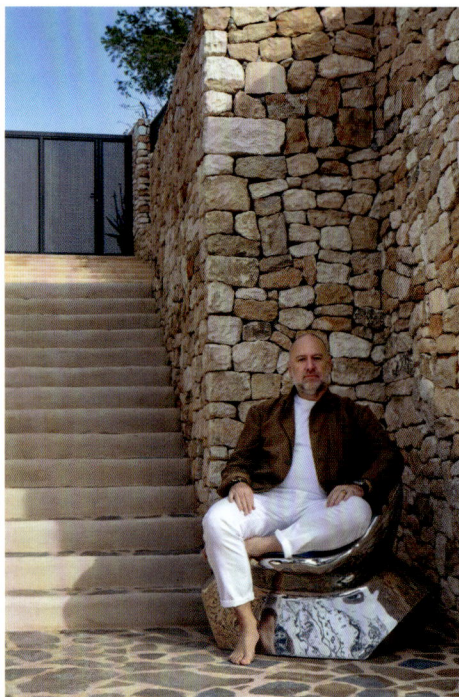

CANE AND ABBA
A classic hanging Egg Chair by Nanna and Jørgen Ditzel hangs from the wooden ceiling, backing on to a pair of Poul Kjærholm for Fritz Hansen steel-framed easy chairs, perfectly positioned to take in the abundance of flora (*opposite*). This is just one of many artfully curated seating areas in the house. A Manuel Marin reinterpretation of an Alexander Calder sculpture perches upon a painted vintage sideboard/credenza and a trio of disco ball crash helmets are at the ready for when an Abba moment strikes.

David's house, built about 20 years ago, is a simple, modernist cube in design. The sweeping porch lends it a Brazilian mid-century vibe that's reminiscent of architect Lina Bo Bardi's masterwork, Casa de Vidro. The original owner's decision to name the house 'Spyglass' adds an intriguing, Bond-like glamour to its story.

David moved here from a gated community in Roca Llisa to satiate his yearning for space, gardens, orchards and privacy while remaining connected to essential locations and cherished communities. He spends much of the island's low season alone or catching up with local friends over intimate meals,

at home or in the glasshouse. In contrast, the summer season is a carousel of hosting friends and pulling together vibrant gatherings with the eclectic folk that live on or frequent the island. David celebrates the duality of this lifestyle and shifts between the 'Hedonistic season of Bes, to the tranquil, restorative season of Tanit' – two gods worshipped here by the Phoenicians – with ease. After years of 'gypsetting', he now values a more contemplative and meaningful life in Ibiza.

David undertook numerous renovations, including uprooting a parched lawn and replacing it with shrubbery. The idyllic gardens hum with wildlife and the scent of flowers. He created an elegant pool salon with a state-of-the-art outdoor kitchen and a large, well-stocked bar to service the raucous summer season. The interior of the house is a museum for his trove of collectibles, antiques, art and important furniture.

Flabbergasted by the island's bureaucracy and planning restrictions, David had to be creative and solution-focused – not a problem for a man who's spent the past 20 years gathering open-source intelligence and working with financial institutions and government agencies. He homed in on the

outdoor living spaces, amplifying all usable areas without touching the house itself. David diligently recycles water from the house – an ingenious approach that is both environmentally and practically driven, given the island's water limitations – and is deeply committed to his daily roaming around his patch of land and year-round swims in the pool. His gratitude for the outdoor spaces, forests and ancient stone terraces is palpable.

The kitchen, though bijou, is perfectly formed, blending traditional and modern styles. Fully intact with the highest-grade appliances, its modest stature can service most events. It segues seamlessly into a series of dining and gathering zones. Objets d'art and ceramics adorn the walls and various surfaces, and David's appetite for life and culture is evident. Efficient shelving systems house his collection of first-edition books, cherished photographs and travel paraphernalia. The main living area is meticulously curated and flows with convivial circularity. The central staircase descends to the restful bedrooms and his study space, all bedecked with impressive antiques, eclectic artworks, indulgent en-suites and life-affirming views.

LA ESQUINA

A timber-framed outdoor furniture set by Michele Bönan, bedecked with graphic motif cushions, creates a restful corner in the open-plan living space (*pages 132–133*). The Ico Parisi circular table in ebonised wood displays a plethora of collectibles. Behind it lie breathtaking views of the island and sea.

SUPER MODULAR

Taichiro Nakai's Modular Bookcase offers cleverly compartmentalised niches that allow for a haphazard display of books and objets d'art (*right*).

BREAKFAST CLUB

A Jens Juul Eilersen chaise in its original cognac leather reclines next to a marble table by Angelo Mangiarotti and a pair of Hans Wegner China chairs (*below and opposite*). A 1950s brass leaf floor lamp by Tommaso Barbi stands beside a Milo Baughman for Thayer Coggin Highboy dresser (*opposite*). A painting by Horacio García Rossi adorns the wall above. Adjacent to the kitchen, this is the perfect spot for breakfast.

TABLE MANNERS
Ico Parisi's ebonised wood table is set for tea and comfortably seats four. The dining chairs are Spanish and date to the 1960s (*left*). An Italian table also dating to the 1960s dominates the central exterior space, surrounded by velvet-clad dining chairs (*below*). A vintage disco ball hangs above, a twinkling reminder of the island's reputation for fun. The 1940s Frederik Stærmose sideboard/credenza holds tableware.

KITCHEN ELEMENTS
A beloved vintage Spanish landscape painting informs the kitchen palette of coppery hues enhanced by Georg Jensen's hanging kitchenware and a trio of rattan bistro stools by Maison Louis Drucker.

'The kitchen segues seamlessly into a series of dining and gathering zones.'

ELEGANCE AT PLAY
Vintage porthole mirrors paired with classical busts upon concrete plinths flank *Leaves – Arrow Weed* by Anton van Dalen. The sofa by Alexis de la Falaise is a vision in rust velvet while William Haines' Slipper chairs offer quiet balance. Studio Superego's Pirite coffee table provides a stirring centrepiece in this opulent scene.

A LIFE WELL TRAVELLED

The guest bedroom displays a cornucopia of global artefacts (*opposite*). A Christian Rosa painting provides an expressive and dynamic backdrop for the Spanish Modernist bench, while an Oceanic Iatmul ancestor mask gazes beatifically into the room, and a Picasso Madoura *Portrait of a Bearded Man* hangs imperiously above.

CRUISE COLLECTION

A roped balustrade and pillars lend the stairwell nautical charm (*right*). Ico Parisi armchairs sit at the helm of the stairwell curve, and a mobile in the style of Alexander Calder shimmies in the breeze.

POOL HOUSE

The pool house is designed to cater for impromptu gatherings and celebrations replete with a pair of saffron hued L-shape sofas on a sheltered loggia, a well-stocked bar and an outdoor kitchen (*pages 142–143*).

OBJECT LESSON

The display of objects is a nuanced practice. For some it's the final touch for a room, while for others it's an opportunity for an ever-evolving tableau of personal expression. I fall into the latter camp. The most obvious starting point for a display is a handful of objects with personal meaning: heirlooms, photographs, ceramics, postcards, artworks: the list is endless. With this cluster of objects, you can set the mood of a room. Personally, I love to pair fine art with a dash of kitsch: a still-life painting beside a pop art sculpture. There's something about the juxtaposition of the sublime and the ridiculous that always creates an interesting focal point.

Placement is crucial: objects shouldn't be perfectly aligned. Hang art at varying heights to avoid the clichéd monotony of a crowded gallery wall. Arrange paintings, records and books on a shelf rather than the usual run of book spines. Symmetry and asymmetry can happily coexist; symmetrical arrangements convey order and tranquillity, while asymmetrical ones are dynamic and modern.

The intentional use of negative space allows a piece to stand out in all its glory. It's the toughest exercise, as the desire to fill space is hard to resist. One object displayed alone can make more of an impact than an entire collection. A plinth or floating shelf can help you achieve this.

Catherine and Jonathan's revamped home is a five-floor end-of-terrace/row house built from brick and timber. It is located between De Beauvoir Town and Canonbury in North-East London, an area known for its bustling community and handsome period properties. This Victorian townhouse is no exception.

POP ART PARADISE

After two decades living in Limehouse, close to the Thames, upsizing to this home was a well-earned upgrade for two City professionals seeking an easy commute and surroundings that resonate with their style. However, an ambitious renovation was needed. Their mission: to transform the property, built circa 1850 and later split into two, to its original glory. Jo Berryman Studio helped consolidate the initial vision alongside Paul Archer Design, which oversaw architecture and build. The back of the house was extended, a basement was excavated and the interior was rebuilt from scratch.

Catherine and Jonathan acquired the house from the Goldfinger estate and its previous owner was the son of famed Hungarian-born architect Ernö Goldfinger, who was the eponymous inspiration behind Ian Fleming's Bond villain. This connection was particularly serendipitous, as the couple enjoyed their first kiss at a 007-themed Christmas party. Suffice to say, Bond is a meaningful part of their life together.

The couple envisioned a playful, open-plan configuration that would provide various zones for entertaining, working and relaxing. Their vision has been realized with minimal compromise on style or quality, despite a significant stretch of budget. The finished interior blends modern and vintage decor, with vivid art and high-end, bespoke pieces of furniture. The multi-layered garden,

a rare jewel so close to central London, is a continuation of the indoor living space, with three distinct areas for different uses.

Upon arrival, visitors are greeted with a themed doormat, a subtle nod to the Goldfinger/Bond connection, while to the left a neon light installation quoting the Persian poet Rumi ('give me wine or leave me alone') is emblazoned across the wall.

The kitchen, designed by the architects, is deliberately minimal and modern. State-of-the-art appliances have been integrated into modular units and there is copious storage. It leads into an intimate dining area

WINDOW SEAT
A bespoke banquette in the original bay window provides a comfortable perch with built-in storage below (*opposite*). Pumpkin-shaped poufs from Soho Home are clustered around a Maisons du Monde coffee table, ready for occasional gatherings. The flooring is reclaimed oak laid in a herringbone pattern.

illuminated by a trio of Parisian street lights (refashioned into pendants) and defined by a lipstick-red feature wall adorned with a painting of Borobudur temple in Java. Pieces of note include artworks by Alice Instone and a bespoke dining table designed by the couple and made by Forest to Home. The living room is an intoxicating mix of modern and pop art, with glossy tomes, curvaceous furniture, sculptural chandeliers and travel memorabilia, including a pair of traditional intricately painted animal skulls from Mexico.

The five bathrooms are luxuriously finished in marble, stone and porcelain. There are three bedrooms upstairs, each with its own unique theme. The main bedroom exudes a feminine softness with its profusion of blush hues and tactile fabrics, while the guest suites on the top floor draw their inspiration from Paris and Ibiza respectively. The moody 'man cave' in the basement can be converted into a fourth bedroom if needed.

Revived by its new owners, today this house represents the perfect union of historic charm and modern luxury.

UNEXPECTED HARMONY

A cheeky electric-blue fringed cabinet by Red Candy sits coquettishly beneath an exquisite hand-painted skull, a folk-art souvenir from Mexico (*above*).

CONVERSATION PIECES

There's nothing linear in this elegant salon. The curvaceous Parrot sofa is by Julian Chichester (*right*). To its right stands a Tommaso Barbi Ginkgo floor lamp from circa 1970. A Damier vase by L'Objet disrupts the scene with a monochrome pop on the Haumea coffee table by Gallotti & Radice.

SHOW ROOM
The reclaimed fireplace was found at Architectural Forum (*left*). *Paris by Day*, an evocative piece by Yvonne Michiels, adorns the chimney breast. Catherine and Jonathan's library of travel books from Assouline radiates colour like a sweet shop, while vintage Yeti club chairs by Jindrich Halabala reupholstered in Icelandic sheepskin look like a pair of living sculptures.

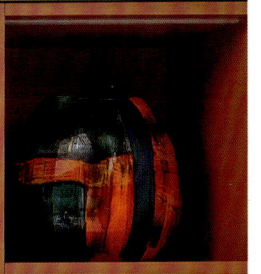

A bespoke modular storage system serves as both a functional piece and gallery wall for various street and pop art sculptures by L'Objet. The sumptuous and yielding sofa from Camerich is ideal for collapsing into at the end of a long day.

FLASH OF INSPIRATION

The bespoke kitchen is minimal and modular (*above*). It has been embellished with metallic flashes such as the copper base cabinet and kick plates and the bistro-inspired bar stools by Seatable.

LIPSTICK ON THE WALL

The kitchen opens onto the dining area, with its bespoke table by Forest to Home and chairs from Rockett St George (*right*). The red wall was inspired by Amy Adams' lip colour in Tom Ford's *Nocturnal Animals*. A Javanese temple painting is framed by a pair of retro table lamps.

BLUSHING BOUDOIR
Cotton-candy pinks define this bedroom (*opposite and this page*). Photographs by Hervé Dunoyer glisten on the wall here and in the marble ensuite. The bed has Bert Frank wall lights integrated into the headboard. An Alpaca rug from The Rug Company is soft underfoot and Giopato & Coombes' Bolle chandelier floats overhead.

FEATURE WALL

A feature wall is a quintessential decorative statement. It has the lofty ability to transform a room's ambience, adding depth and character without over-egging the decorative pudding. Highlighting one wall with a distinct colour, texture or material will disrupt monotony and delineate space within open-plan layouts. Darker tones make a room appear more intimate and moody, while lighter or brighter ones elicit a sense of openness and vitality. It's an effective design hack, anchoring furniture arrangements and accentuating architectural features or a burgeoning art collection.

On the flipside, the feature wall is an opportunity to take curation into your own hands and defy the rules of conformity and taste. It is a surface on which to mount chaos and emotional bric-à-brac. Every home needs one. It's a shrine, in the non-denominational sense of the word.

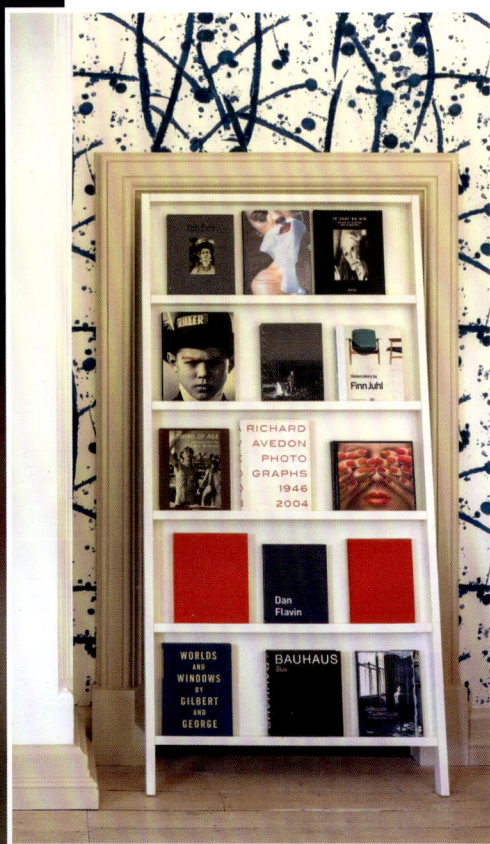

An area where moments and events can be recorded. A celebration of day-to-day divinity. Children's artwork, concert tickets, invitations, scribbled notes, postcards, passport photos and shopping lists. In the past I've even designated a 'dirt wall' in a home for the children (and grown-ups) to perfect handstands and for general mark-making. There's a beauty and temporality to scuffs and scrawls: it's very BE HERE NOW.

HANDSEWN BY THE SEA

Ensconced on the Kentish coast is a home that blends retro charm with do-it-yourself brawn. Everything within has been either repurposed, reclaimed, handmade or pilfered from a skip/dumpster, proving that great design needn't cost the earth. What's more, the house is a mere 20-minute meander from door to sea.

HEARTH AND SOUL
Layered rugs bring comfort and warmth to the stripped floorboards and delineate between the living and dining area within the open-plan layout (*opposite left*). The open fireplace is the life and soul of the house (*opposite right*). A Heinz Mayochup poster for a Katherine Bernhardt and José Luis Vargas exhibition adorns the chimney breast, setting a playful and irreverent tone. A mid-century sideboard/credenza has been painted in a glossy egg-yolk yellow and doubles up as a vinyl library.

Alexandra Mann, a freelance red-carpet stylist and costume designer, lives here with her wine merchant partner. They previously lived in rented accommodation in London for over 25 years, but when they entered the market to buy, the inevitable draw of more 'bang for their buck' took hold. Friends in and around Thanet and Deal waxed lyrical about the community spirit and cultural buzz of the area and soon Alexandra and her partner discovered their new home, a rough-cut gem with potential in spades.

The house was built in the early 1900s, but had a pebble-dashed facade and a 1970s interior preserved in aspic: veneer panels, woodchip wallpaper, highly flammable ceiling tiles and thick-ply shag carpet. Much of its original character had been forfeited over time, including fireplaces and original Crittall windows. The stoical former owner had lived without central heating or double glazing, so the shell was spartan and archaic. Undoing had to commence before any doing could be done, and an intensive strip-out ensued.

I've known Alexandra for years, and she has the tenacity to make anything work. Budget constraints heavily influenced the renovation, but amplified her creativity. A new roof, rewiring, installation of a boiler and radiators were the first priorities. Removing the woodchip wallpaper was challenging; steaming it off was a threat to the original lath-and-plaster walls, necessitating a full reboard.

To manage costs, Alexandra would frequent auctions and scour eBay and Freecycle. Jackpot finds include original wooden shutters, a claw-foot bathtub, unwanted furniture from film sets and a red-carpet stair runner. The bijou garden is an overgrown splendour of verdant grass, sunny dandelions and an established rose bush. It's a seamless adjunct to the living space and a wild backdrop for an antique Bierkeller table, which serves as a second dining room all year round.

The front door opens into a hallway furnished with French abattoir hooks for coats and a circus-tent striped curtain to insulate against coastal gusts. The utilities are hidden by a box made from old fruit crates by artisan Rocky Alvarez, who also had a hand in the Spanish-style kitchen next door. This space is defined by natural materials and repurposed antiques: iroko-wood school lab benches, a gargantuan reclaimed butler's sink and a porcelain draining board sourced at auction. Rocky constructed the sink support from

school gym bars, and even the wall shelf was once a church pew. It's a highly functional space, perfect for cooking and entertaining.

The open-plan living and dining area is as intimate as it is eclectic. A Victorian metal trestle table with an old door serves for mealtimes and for pattern-cutting. The living area includes two street-found wooden armchairs, a large floor cushion (handsewn by Alexandra) and a gallery wall featuring works by Juliette Blightman and Lucy Sparrow. A Warhol *Cow* print and assorted objets trouvés bring in more wit and high art.

In the main bedroom, an Ikea mirrored wardrobe/armoire meets a sugary pink 1960s chest of drawers/dresser gifted by Alexandra's mum. The bathroom is equally charming, featuring a rosy-hued glass ceiling light repurposed as a console basin and a Victorian claw-foot tub, all enveloped in the soothing tones of Farrow & Ball's Peignoir. Alexandra, not yet finished, is already plotting its makeover in glossy lipstick-red.

TREASURES FOUND
The couple are avid collectors of colourful ceramics, curios, books and art. The living area's Victorian shutters were found at auction. An architectural pillar adds a nautical edge to the scene.

COOKING FOR A CROWD
In the kitchen, staggered staging elevates the cooking area and a window looks out onto the lush garden (*this page*). The rug is from Morocco. Alexandra loves to cook and her partner is a wine merchant, so naturally they throw great dinner parties.

DOOR-TO-DOOR DINING
The dining table is an old door resting on Victorian trestles (*opposite*). The chairs are mid-century classics, some by Ercol and others by Carlo Bartoli for Kartell. One of Alexandra's bespoke kaftans hangs from the window frame.

CANDY FLOSS

WATER WORKS

A Victorian claw-foot tub, reconditioned by the couple, strikes a pleasing contrast with the bathroom's chequered linoleum flooring (*right*). A sweet ochre tub chair is poised to receive towels and dressing gowns/bathrobes.

VIVID VIGNETTES

Tuinol Barry, Chelsea, London (1981), an arresting photograph by Derek Ridgers, greets you at the top of the stairs (*below*). On top of the cabinet are a 1950s ice-cream print, a Lego floral bouquet and a pair of disco-dancing rainbow-hued Christian Louboutins.

MAKING THE BED

The cushions atop the bed are all handmade by Alexandra, who rotates the covers seasonally (*opposite*). Peignoir by Farrow & Ball is a calming backdrop for the riot of colour.

'Alexandra has the tenacity to make anything work – budget constraints amplified her creativity.'

COMBINING COLOURS

Combining colours is like throwing together the perfect salad. Imagine each leaf teetering on the edge of bitterness until you drizzle it with a honey-mustard dressing. As you toss, the flavours meld together, transforming it into something savoury, sweet and utterly delicious. That's my style: a bit of honey mustard.

I love blending unexpected shades or contrasting prints. Intuition often takes the lead, but over time I've honed my skill to strike just the right balance of contrasting elements. Imagine a Louis XIV bed on a magenta shag-pile rug in a lacquered-black room. Or a futuristic Arne Jacobsen Egg chair reupholstered in a Sanderson floral. These hybrids elevate each other, creating something more substantial and enduring.

Colours have the power to evoke feelings and memories. Deep emerald and ripe plum are perfect for a library or study, where they will encourage introspection and thoughtful discourse. Bright egg-yolk yellow or peppermint green inject a burst of energy, sparking lively banter in kitchens and dining rooms. And putty pink or sky blue is calming and restful in the bedroom or hallway.

Colour combinations can have a practical function, too. Colour blocking is useful for defining zones in a small room or carving out intimate pockets in big open-plan spaces.

Fiona Dewson knew that 'This house could take colour.' Reimagining her elegant townhouse in North London was a journey that Jo Berryman Studio and Stephen Brandes Architects helped her to navigate.

TECHNICOLOR TERRACE

As a designer, it's not every day I am given the opportunity to remodel a stately and well-proportioned Regency townhouse. But Fiona had performed her due diligence and knew that the sort of interiors I deliver are far from the school of greige. She also happens to be the epitome of chic and the possessor of a well-honed design eye herself.

Along with her family, Fiona had lived in this Grade II-listed house for seven years before plunging into major renovation work, undertaken in order to allow the family, which includes her financier husband and their three children, to adapt their home to meet their

changing needs. My brief included converting the existing first-floor drawing room into a master bedroom suite to facilitate the creation of four en-suite bedrooms on the upper floors for the children and guests.

The refurbishment also involved opening up the lower ground floor by replacing an old extension with a double-height glazed insertion that incorporates a glass balcony, now an office space for Fiona. The ground floor is home to a formal drawing room and a library-cum-study, while a cute, cocoon-like snug on the first floor offers an entertainment and chill zone for the teenagers.

Working alongside a client who is open to suggestions and up for a complete overhaul is a designer's dream. And, despite expressing some initial doubts, Fiona totally came out as colour-amorous. The house showcases an idiosyncratic blend of hues and patterns that could seem overwhelming at first glance. However, once the eyes have settled and full absorption of the ambience has set in, it's easy to appreciate how seamlessly the surroundings flow. The family room on the lower ground floor exemplifies this, boasting an acid yellow geometric wing chair, a flower-bomb rug and a sofa in an unusual spirulina-

Foxed mirrored panels and a gold reflective console by Dominic Schuster adorn the hall walls (*opposite*). A trio of alabaster pendant lights and demi-lune sconces by Atelier Alain Ellouz add ethereal illumination. Beneath the dado, a tarnished effect metallic damask wallpaper by Arte subdues the bling (*below*). This works beautifully with Farrow & Ball's Cornforth White on the walls, a perfect backdrop for period features and an eclectic art display.

green looped weave. The eclectic mix is balanced with a pale coral ottoman and a powder-blue lounge chair.

Fiona and her family wanted to showcase their extensive and growing art collection, and a key component of the brief was to carefully select designs and tones that complemented the art, including a contemporary reinterpretation of *The Birth of Venus* that adorns the living-room wall. The Nordic blue polished plaster finish is the perfect backdrop for such vivid pieces and the impressive orb-like lantern hanging from the ceiling adds edge to the room's stately grandeur.

Some choices may have seemed a little too daring at first, such as a gold-mirrored console in the entrance hall, but I tempered the effect by pairing it with a tarnished metallic damask wallpaper and aged mirrored panels. The alabaster moon lights add ethereal softness. The key to design longevity lies in the combination of classical architecture and the use of robust materials such as fumed oak, antiqued bronze and natural stone.

The main bedroom is a haven of comfort and tactility, dressed in luxurious materials including a bespoke silk and wool carpet and soft devoré velvets. Its decor, inspired by a 1920s French gouache of Parisian entertainer Mistinguett, maintains a nuanced yet connected feel with the rest of the house. We incorporated built-in shelving in the room, which allows for curated displays of books, objets, family photos and art.

Fiona's home is truly a dynamic and active space that reflects the perpetual evolution of life and family. A little bit of design daring has gone a long way, and this home is proof that brave interior choices can foster a cohesive and harmonious living environment.

NORDIC BLUES
The movie *The Danish Girl* was the inspiration for the Nordic blue scheme in the living room (*left and above*). The walls are hand-rendered in polished plaster while the floors are fumed oak. A reinterpretation of *The Birth of Venus* by Will Tuck hangs above an Amy Somerville blue velvet sofa. An olive-hued 1950s Danish sofa sits in the window, while an original Willy Rizzo coffee table offers a metallic gleam. An ostrich-plumed floor lamp by A Modern Grand Tour stands in the corner and the Bethan Gray cocktail console adds a coral twist.

BREAKFAST AT TIFFANYS
The kitchen is by Boffi. The breakfast bar stools are clad in Tiffany blue pleather and the Celestial Pebble light is by Ochre.

DINNER CIRCLE
In the dining room, the wallpaper is from Arte, the table is by Rupert Bevan and the chairs are Dooq (*opposite*). The Bolle chandelier is by Giopato & Coombes. An exquisite floral sculpture by by Harumi Klossowska de Rola (Balthus' daughter) glistens in the centre.

SPIRULINA SMOOTHIE
An artwork of
Repton Boxing
Club by Brigitte
Smith inspired the
palette in the
family room.
A capacious
Standard sofa by
Edra in a glorious
spirulina-hued
looped fabric takes
centre stage, the
floral rug is by
artist Jan Kath and
the ottoman is
clad in buttoned
coral pleather
alongside an
eau-de-Nil Pierre
Paulin Pumpkin
chair for Ligne
Roset. This space
doubles up as a
cinema room.

GOGGLEBOX
The snug is a teen dream (*left*). A comfy L-shape sofa in a persimmon velvet and dense shagpile rug provide textured comfort. The coloured glass apothecary bottles are by Dutch brand Polspotten.

LIGHT EXPLOSION
An original 1960s Sputnik chandelier seems to defy gravity above the stairwell; almost more of a sculptural piece than a light fixture (*below*).

WABI SABI
Finely fractured gesso wardrobe doors create an elegant corridor to the bathroom, which is clad in marble interspersed with decorative tiles that echo the eau-de-Nil hues in the adjoining bedroom. The Iceland bath is by Boffi.

'This home is proof that brave interior choices can foster a cohesive and harmonious living environment.'

A 1927 gouache of French actress and chanteuse Mistinguett sets the tone for the main bedroom (*opposite*). The walls are wallpapered in Travertine in Halley by Fromental and the bespoke carpet is by Tai Ping. Devoré velvet curtains are finished with pelmets in chartreuse velvet, while an armchair by Porada is dressed with a cushion by Silken Favours. The trio of circular pendants is from Cameron Design House (*this page*). The curvaceous headboard combines ruched velvet and dusky paisley by de Le Cuona.

TEXTURE OVERLAY

Contrasting textures is my failsafe solution whenever I feel a design block. I task myself with imagining unlikely texture pairings, colour choices or groupings of objects. It's the opposite of Tetris, where the objective is for everything to slot together tidily – the idea behind texture overlay is to surprise and confound. I use it as a technique to add depth, break up bland interiors and inject a note of the unexpected.

Achieve a sense of textural contrast by combining contrasting fabrics like buttery leather or cut velvet in a design statement – a leather trim around a woollen cushion, or a suede headboard with velvet buttoning. A raw plaster wall provides the perfect backdrop for glossy black and white photography. Floral motifs in acid tones add zest to a pared-back backdrop of subtle tonal colours, as does a glittering disco ball suspended from a rustic beam.

Colour can play its part in adding a sense of depth too. If a room's base tone is smoky tobacco or deepest aubergine, introduce a flash of metallic paper, a plume of feathers or a neon art installation to achieve a spot of visual disruption.

Vintage textures are innately more storied, so try to bring these into your home. A reclaimed wood floor provides a weathered, imperfect surface that will temper the sleek, sculptural lines of modern furniture. Soften parquet flooring, mirrors or panelled walls with a layering of gauzy materials such as silk, taffeta, satin and velvet to infuse a design scheme with a sense of theatre; think Marie Antoinette-like opulence spliced with 21st-century furnishings.

SOURCES

Here's a guide to where you might find some of the items shown in this book or similarly bold and beautiful pieces that will make your home sing.

SURFACES, WALLCOVERINGS AND FABRICS

1838 Wallcoverings

1830wallcoverings.com
A collection of decorative papers from the V&A archive reinterpreted for modern homes.

Bert & May

bertandmay.com
Handcrafted zellige tiles in a rainbow of colours.

de Gournay

degournay.com
Exquisite handpainted wallpaper and fabrics.

Divine Savages

divinesavages.com
Glamorous wallpapers and fabrics from Jamie Watkins and Tom Kennedy, whose home features on *pages 52–65*.

Inspired Metal

inspiredmetal.co.uk
Copper surfaces and hoods like the one in my kitchen on *pages 14–15*.

Timorous Beasties

timorousbeasties.com
Fascinating and surreal patterns on wallpapers, fabric and cushions.

Wendy Morrison

wendymorrisondesign.com
Maximalist wallpaper and rugs plus fabulous fabrics, as seen in Wendy's home on *pages 40–49*.

Watson & Gabb

watsonandgabb.com
Specialist finishes, including resin and liquid metal.

FURNITURE

Amy Somerville

amysomerville.com
Elegant and unusual furniture and textiles made to order.

Bethan Gray

bethangray.com
Colourful and luxurious statement furniture.

Casa Botelho

casabotelho.com
Furniture that makes your heart beat faster, as seen on *pages 28–36*.

Forest to Home

foresttohome.co.uk
Solid timber handcrafted dining tables and more.

Rose Uniacke

roseuniacke.com
Beautiful pieces.

Soho Home

sohohome.com
Contemporary furniture, textiles and lighting.

Triptych Furniture

triptychfurniture.com
Inventive and unusual bespoke furniture.

LIGHTING

CTO Lighting

cto.lighting.co.uk
Many of the statement lights in my home were sourced here.

Ochre

ochre.net
Timeless and elegant contemporary lighting.

Schwung Design

Schwung.design
Dramatic light fittings, as seen in the home of João Botelho on *pages 28–37*.

Tigermoth Lighting Ltd

Tigermothlighting.com
Sculptural lighting.

Tom Dixon

tomdixon.net
Bold statement lighting and furniture.

ANTIQUES AND VINTAGE

Alfies Antiques Market

13-25 Church Street
London NW8 8DT
alfiesantiques.com
Look here for modern classic furniture.

Aquarius Vintage

@aquarius.vintage
One of a kind vintage treasures.

Chairish

charish.com
A curated online marketplace shipping within the United States.

French Finds

frenchfinds.co.uk
Quality antique French furniture and accessories.

Pamono

pamono.co.uk
A stylish array of mid-century and vintage finds.

Sigmar London

Sigmarlondon.com
Carefully curated original modernist furniture.

The Vintage Hub

thevintagehub.com
Mid-century and vintage pieces.

Vinterior

vinterior.co
Vintage and mid-century pieces from all over Europe shipped to your door.

ART

Abstract House

abstracthouse.com
Art prints and abstract paintings with presence.

The Ancient Home

theancienthome.com
Classical Greek and Roman busts.

King & McGaw

kingandmcgaw.com
Eyecatching fine art prints, including XL pieces for additional impact.

Mccully & Crane

mccullyandcrane.com
Joyful and inspiring original art.

ACCESSORIES

Abigail Ahern

abigailahearn.com
Accessories, lighting and furniture with attitude.

Anissa Kermiche

anissakermiche.com
Cheeky pots and accessories.

Beards & Daisies

beardsanddaisies.co.uk
A great array of large houseplants.

Beauvamp Studio

beauvamp.com
Glorious vintage-inspired lampshades with ruffles, scallops and fringes.

Beldi Rugs

beldirugs.com
Experts in Moroccan Berber rugs.

Coco & Wolf

cocoandwolf.com
Dreamy bedding in an array of Liberty prints.

Etsy.com

A place where you will find many of the decorative accents shown in this book, including disco ball helmets, Iatmul masks, painted skulls, vintage lighting, kitsch ceramics, rocket lamps, and more.

A Rum Fellow

arumfellow.com
Bold and beautiful rugs, fabrics and cushions.

PICTURE CREDITS

KEY: **a** = above; **b** = below; **l** = left; **c** = centre; **r** = right

1 The home of interior designer and creative director Jo Berryman; **2** The home of designer Wendy Morrison in Scotland, www.wendymorrisondesign.com; **3 c** The home of Fiona Goldberg; **4** The home of David Leppan; **5** The home of interior designer and creative director Jo Berryman; **6** The home of Jamie Watkins & Tom Kennedy of design house Divine Savages, www.divinesavages.com; **7-27 al** The home of interior designer and creative director Jo Berryman; **27 r** The home of Jonathan & Catherine, North London; **28-38** Casa Botelho, casabotelho.com; **39** The home of interior designer and creative director Jo Berryman; **40-49** The home of designer Wendy Morrison in Scotland, www.wendymorrisondesign.com; **50 ar** The home of Rosie & Oliver, Hampstead, London; **50 b** The home of artist Alice Instone near Rye, England; **51 a** The home of designer Wendy Morrison in Scotland, www.wendymorrisondesign.com; **51 br** The home of artist Alice Instone near Rye, England; **52-65** The home of Jamie Watkins & Tom Kennedy of design house Divine Savages, www.divinesavages.com; **66 al** The home of interior designer and creative director Jo Berryman; **66 ar** The home of Rosie & Oliver, Hampstead, London; **66 bl-67** The home of Jamie Watkins & Tom Kennedy of design house Divine Savages, www.divinesavages.com; **68-77** The home of Jasmine Hemsley, wellbeing expert and author, and Nick Hopper, photographer and creative director; **78 al** The home of interior designer and creative director Jo Berryman; **78 ar** The home of Jasmine Hemsley, wellbeing expert and author, and Nick Hopper, photographer and creative director; **79 al** The home of interior designer and creative director Jo Berryman; **79 bl** The home of Jonathan & Catherine, North London; **79 r** The home of Jasmine Hemsley, wellbeing expert and author, and Nick Hopper, photographer and creative director; **80-96** The home of Sophie Daunais; **97 al** Casa Botelho, casabotelho.com; **97 ar** The home of David Leppan; **97 b** The home of Sophie Daunais; **98-107** The home of Rosie & Oliver, Hampstead, London; **108 ar** The home of David Leppan; **108 bl** & **109** The home of Rosie & Oliver, Hampstead, London; **110-128 ac** & **ar** The home of artist Alice Instone near Rye, England; **128 bl** The home of Fiona Goldberg; **129 al** & **bl** The home of designer Wendy Morrison in Scotland, www.wendymorrisondesign.com; **129 r** The home of Jamie Watkins & Tom Kennedy of design house Divine Savages, www.divinesavages.com; **130-144 bl** The home of David Leppan; **144 br** The home of Jonathan & Catherine, North London; **145** The home of Fiona Goldberg; **146-158 ar** The home of Jonathan & Catherine, North London; **158 bl** The home of interior designer and creative director Jo Berryman; **159 al** & **ar** The home of Jonathan & Catherine, North London; **159 b** The home of David Leppan; **160-167** The home of costume designer/stylist Alexandra Mann, Kent Coast, www.alexandramann.com; **168 al** The home of interior designer and creative director Jo Berryman; **168 ar** The home of costume designer/stylist Alexandra Mann, Kent Coast, www.alexandramann.com; **168 br** The home of designer Wendy Morrison in Scotland, www.wendymorrisondesign.com; **169 l** The home of interior designer and creative director Jo Berryman; **169 ar** & **br** The home of costume designer/stylist Alexandra Mann, Kent Coast, www.alexandramann.com; **170-181** The home of Fiona Goldberg; **182 a** The home of artist Alice Instone near Rye, England; **182 bl, br** & **183 l** The home of Fiona Goldberg; **183 r** The home of Jonathan & Catherine, North London; **185** Casa Botelho, casabotelho.com; **186** & **189** The home of Rosie & Oliver, Hampstead, London; **190-191** The home of interior designer and creative director Jo Berryman; **192** The home of Jamie Watkins & Tom Kennedy of design house Divine Savages, www.divinesavages.com; **Endpapers** The home of designer Wendy Morrison in Scotland, www.wendymorrisondesign.com.

ACKNOWLEDGMENTS

I dedicate this book to my children, my partner Philip and mum Monette. Without your love and continuous cheerleading, I wouldn't have been able to travel, write or wrangle my thoughts.

Deepest respect and gratitude to Rachel Ashwell, who saw potential in my idea. You're an indomitable force and source of inspiration. So happy we're neighbours.

A huge exhale and megawatt 'Thank you' to Annabel Morgan, Leslie Harrington et al at Ryland Peters & Small/ CICO books. You took a punt on my vision. Without your support and expertise, the delivery of this book would have been impossible.

Thank you to Bénédicte Drummond, who nails the visual language of *Expressive Interiors* with her stunning photography. You're a joy to work with.

Thank you too to the talented Sihem Mornas, who styles the scenes impeccably. You are gold.

Thank you to my former colleagues Javier Garcia-Alzorriz and Molly Isaacs for your loyalty and dedication to Jo Berryman Studio – miss you guys. Thank you to my current colleague Michelle Harris for holding down the fort in my absence. Thank you to Vaughan Rogers and Daisy Bird for fortuitous introductions. Thank you to Piotr Kosciukiewicz for all his building prowess and materials knowledge on many of my projects.

Finally, I'd like to personally thank João, Wendy, Jamie, Tom, Jasmine, Nick, Sophie, Rosie, Oliver, Alice, Hugh, David, Catherine, Jon, Alexandra, Charles, Fiona and Hedley, for generously opening up your homes and being such wonderful collaborators. I hope you love how we've captured your authenticity and expressive souls.

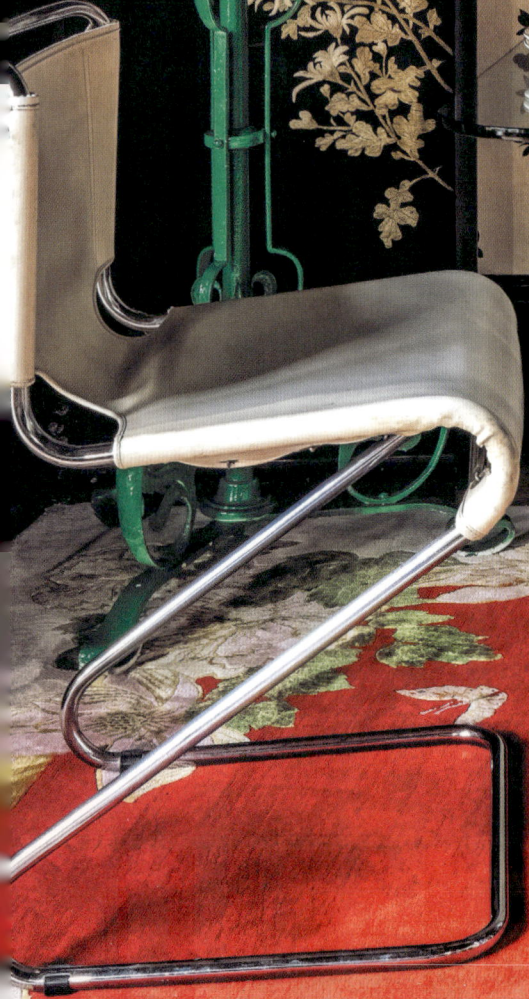